Be Heard To Be Rich

About the Book

Author Mighty Pete Lonton shares the lessons he has learned and the insights he has gained through some 400 guest interviews in over 1,000 hours in the first year of the 'Fire in the Belly' Show and podcast. Mighty Pete shares how we can show that we are listening and know that we are being heard which is one of the core values for us as human beings - we need and want connection and love for ourselves and others.

He shares his findings that, for himself and many of the guests on the show, it is in going within and hearing ourselves that we can raise our levels of consciousness to be rich in all areas of life. Mighty Pete will show you how and help you to reflect on your own inner genius.

The hypothesis of this book is that we all have a fire and genius inside us. The beautiful fact of life is that we are all on different stages of the journey.

Also available as an eBook and Audiobook
Visit MightyPete.com

From the Author

If you are feeling unheard in life, or are constantly being told that you are not listening by those around you, if you find that you are unable to or have stopped listening to yourself, read this book, Be Heard to Be Rich.

Be heard or die - How can being heard save lives? This is the point at which from great overwhelm can come great change for many people. Change may be necessary when you decide that good is not good enough and the status quo is not the path or the blueprint for your future. The seeds for your future lie within you but it is up to you to nurture them and let them take hold.

Being Heard is the path to Being Rich. In this context your 'Being' is your inner most true self that is selfishly complete and is the moral compass by which you are guided. It is this inner most true self that needs to be heard. Many will see the word 'rich' and interpret it as the material trappings of life, but here I am referring to the seeds of love, joy, opportunity and potential within every one of us.

Learn how to hear and be heard if you want to be rich in life, deepen your connections, create success, build wealth, and find joy, love, peace of mind and happiness. Whatever you are looking for, learning how to hear ourselves, and others enables us to listen to our inner genius and is critical to your life's journey and your soul's purpose of finding itself.'

Mighty Pete Lonton

Endorsement for Be Heard to Be Rich:

'You can now HEAR your way to riches and an
ever brighter and better future,'

-   **Mark Victor Hansen**

Worldwide Bestselling Author, Co-Author of the Chicken Soup for the
Soul series, Co-Author of Ask! Mark has sold over 500 Million books
worldwide.

First Published in 2021 by Fire In The Belly Publishing

Pete Lonton has asserted his right to be identified as the Author of this Work has been asserted in accordance with the Copyright, Designs and Patent Act 1988 and Intellectual Property (Copyright and Related Rights) (EU Exit) (Amendment etc) Regulations 2019.

ISBN: 978-1-8383820-2-5

Fire In The Belly Publishing
MightyPete.com

Be Heard To Be Rich

Listen to Your Inner Genius
How being heard can change lives

By Pete Lonton

Fire In The Belly Publishing

This book is dedicated to all those who haven't been heard, yet

Just know that we are all perfectly imperfect and that's okay

This book accompanies **'Is Your Inner Genius Being Heard? Find Your Fire'** a TEDx Talk by Mighty Pete Lonton
TEDxDerryLondonderry February 2021

Contents

Chapter One

Be Heard or Die

'The purpose of your life is to be on your journey and not worry about the destination. Find and live your Fire in the Belly.'

Be Heard to Be Rich? How can being heard make me rich? What does rich mean to you?

If you want to be rich in life, learning how to hear and be heard is the way to deepen your connections, create success, build wealth and find joy, love, peace of mind and happiness.

I plummeted into what I now call my 'mid-life opportunity'. Unable to hear, think, listen or see, I felt like I was dying and out of control. I felt like an imposter and that I was one of the supporting characters in the movie reel of my own life. I had no sense of being the driving force in the life that I was living and felt that I did not really know anything about myself. I, like so many, who reach this type of crisis had stopped listening to myself, it wasn't just that I didn't hear, I had stopped asking; I had stopped talking.

It was time to hear myself - to go within and listen. I had found, in the words of Dr Gabor Maté, the need for 'compassionate self-inquiry.' I found this extremely challenging to start with. To listen, to be able to hear and to quieten the noise in my head. I had to go beyond my mind. I found that I had to listen from my gut, my intuition.

When we say to go within and listen, *do you understand what this means?* In this book we are referring to the narrator, the inner critic, the judge, the voice or voices that keep you company from the moment you wake up to the point you go to sleep. It is the voice of your subconscious mind.

Ask yourself this question – as you read this, where is the voice coming from in your head?

Hearing both myself and others slowly became my focus, my purpose, and ultimately has now become my mission in life. It has led me to find my passion, my 'fire in the belly' and, through founding the Fire In the Belly podcast, to listen to the life stories, insights and lessons of some 400 people in its first year alone.

I heard myself and I have chosen to hear others. I have learned a great deal about not only how to listen, but how to hear, and the impact of being heard on myself and others. It may sound extreme, but I have learned that ultimately the outcome of not being heard can be death. If we don't truly hear what is going on inside us, we allow ourselves and what matters most to us to die.

If we do not hear our body, we may literally die from illness or neglect. If we do not hear our minds, we may not literally die but we may find we are not really living because of feelings of depression or despair. If we do not hear others, we may lose relationships and connections with the people who matter to us. In short, if we do not hear ourselves, we lose ourselves.

'Knowing oneself comes from attending with compassionate curiosity to what is happening within.'

-     **Dr Gabor Maté**

A moment of enlightenment

By truly hearing ourselves and others we have the opportunity to strengthen feelings of connection and relationship. According to Harvard Health Publishing and Harvard Medical School, a 2019 review of dozens of studies showed that good connections and social support can improve health and increase longevity. Connection and close relationships are consistently listed as the most important predictors of health and well-being in global research.

In order to hear others we need to create space, ask questions, and allow the answers to come. In this book I will outline what I have learned and how I have improved my ability to hear. But first I would like to share some of my story and the paths that I have taken to come to understand the power of being heard.

From great overwhelm comes great change

My journey to find my fire *almost* started at a Tony Robbins event – Unleash the Power Within - in April 2017. It was at this event, at 37 and a half years of age that I first heard the expression 'through great overwhelm comes great change'. For me this phrase sums up what turned out to be a massive turning point in terms of my state of mind, my physical health, my finances and pretty much every other area of my life. I found myself in a room with 10,000 plus other people who all wanted to make a massive positive change in their life, for whatever reason. The event was deliberately overwhelming in terms of the lights, the sound, the dancing, the hugging and chanting. For me, as someone who had been a teenager in the 1990s, it felt like a rave – there was a lot of music, a lot of jumping around and I became immersed in the environment. I've since learned that that immersion helps you to bypass the conscious mind and ultimately get to your 'natural frequency'. Along with the dance music and the high energy atmosphere, everyone was being told to go look inside and ask deep questions, that I suggest you consider, including:

'What is it that I would love to do?'

and

'Why am I here?'

During this process of being asked questions, suddenly I found answers started to come up within me. I discovered I wanted to change, and found that I was able to listen and hear myself again. This, I now believe, is key for many of us.

Once I started to hear myself at that event, I went home and started to have breakthrough after breakthrough and realisation after realisation. I started seeking mentors and like-minded people who would listen to me, so that I could explore and process all that I was learning. I began to feel free again and as I met new challenges, found myself wanting to question more deeply my own truths and beliefs rather than numbly just accepting and not questioning.

My perception of my circumstances prior to my 'mid-life opportunity' began to change. Previously, when I looked back at certain events I would think: *'that was a terrible experience'.* But, as I started to create space for myself and learned to stop judging myself, my perception became; *'actually that was a learning experience, I'm glad it wasn't any worse than it was'.* I started to go within, to question myself because I wanted to hear the answers to important questions such as *'what have I learned from this?'* and *'how can I move forward?'* The answers to these questions have led ultimately to the creation of the 'Fire in the Belly' show and podcast. On the show it is my intention to hear people's life stories and in so doing to build rapport and respect for others, and allow the people I interview and the people listening to find their 'fire in the belly'. An important part of this is that the people I interview feel that they are in control and know that the podcast is being recorded in a safe environment - the interviews are pre-recorded and won't be aired unless the guest consents. It is also vitally important that people feel at ease and able to take the time to answer questions fully; so that they can explain themselves and don't feel under pressure. There is also no 'agenda'. As a result I don't think I've ever had a question not answered, or a person feel unable to share their view or perception openly.

It's very much *'let's just grab a comfy chair here and have a chat'* albeit a chat that aims to go much deeper than most.

And that's the style I like to get across. I think that style helps people to go beyond their ego and fears – i.e. get the 'chimp' to go away – (and yes I do see the ego as a chimp, it can be mild-mannered but also aggressive and confrontational...more on that later) - and gets people relaxed and able to look back in a calm and reflective way whilst observing their own journey from a bird's eye view. That calm voice can help us to hear over the loudest shout. Again, that's listening, for me, on so many levels. I want to be able to hear the whisper of the things unsaid. Guests often say that they haven't talked like that before, that they haven't taken the time and haven't been listened to in such a long time, if ever.

That is really important to me. What I have come to understand is the gift in listening - the fact that there is truly power in being heard. So, during the interview process, we find an open space to allow that 'I am' and 'You Are'. If we consider how do we communicate? I believe that being given the opportunity to speak freely and be really heard lets our souls breathe. There is an expression someone used on an interview, which I loved – *'We're basically all souls in a meat suit'.* I want to let our souls get some air.

That's it.

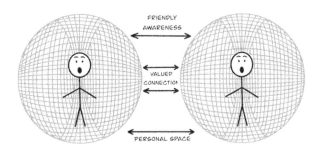

All Souls in a Meat Suit

Who are you? For many years I attached labels to myself an others. For example, I would say 'I'm a father', 'I'm a husband', 'I'm an entrepreneur', I'm this and I'm that. We are also different things to different people and this draws out different parts of our character. *Are you the same person with your life partner as you are with a school friend? Are you the same with a work colleague as a member of your family?* While these labels are all things that you can attach to yourself, they do not describe who you really are. I want to go beyond the labels. To do that you need to go into a seriously deep conversation and that is what I aim to do with my guests in the Fire in the Belly interviews.

I want to hear why somebody lives their life the way they do, there is often a string of questions that we often ask ourselves and like to explore on the show. Questions like; *How do you perceive the world? What do you show me by the way that you communicate? What lessons have you learned along the way? Are you where you are supposed to be now? How will your past affect your future? Does it need to? How do you see your future? What is your overall purpose for your future?*

I believe that in general I'm fairly measured and speak fairly softly: in our house raised voices and arguments stand out. They're unusual. That was also the experience I had in my family growing up. For other people talking loudly or shouting is a normal method of communication. I'm not saying that's right or wrong; it's just different. Whereas, in our house, if someone raises their voice it's an exceptional event and a cue to look at what has happened.

When someone feels they are not being listened to, they might say, 'you're not listening to me,' or ask, 'are you listening to me?' If that doesn't work they may then feel they have no option but to change their method of communication to try to be heard. That can result in silence, shouting, banging on a door, walking off, huffing or doing something else outside of the norm to communicate 'you're not hearing me'. Often what is really going on is that when someone doesn't feel 'heard', they believe that their values are being ignored or not being met by the other person. If you live your life long enough without paying attention to your values or if you are surrounded by people whose values aren't aligned with yours and those people take no interest in understanding your values, ultimately results in people feeling discomfort or dis-ease.

Nine times out of 10 people think that everyone cares what everyone else is doing or saying. They generally don't; they care about themselves and how they are feeling. There's nothing wrong with that in itself. We all have our own views. But, what I have learned is that we want to be seen, we want to be heard, we want to be felt and to be appreciated and valued, to know that our thoughts and opinions matter. *How annoying can it be when someone clearly isn't listening?* Or have you found that maybe you should be taking your own advice. So when we find that we are not heard, or we aren't properly hearing ourselves, we have an opportunity to ask questions of ourselves and others that, if we can hear the answers to, can help us to progress.

The silent tantrum

At 37 and half years old I got to the stage where I was burned out. You could call it midlife crisis, or possibly a form of depression. I say possibly because I've definitely had depression twice in my life and this wasn't the same. It felt more like frustration; like a child's tantrum. By comparing it to a child's tantrum, I do not intend to belittle it or pour shame on myself. But, in the same way that a child might tantrum when it needs or wants something and no-one is listening, I felt that I had something to say but I wasn't being heard.

However, *unlike* a child's tantrum, my adult tantrum was silent. Silence can be the loudest scream. I didn't know where to turn; I felt frightened and in a chaotic almost primal state, feeling that I was totally all over the place and that nobody was listening to me – not even myself.

I have since found that when I actually started to listen to myself I was able to hear that silent tantrum, to recognise my feelings, and consciously back myself down a bit from the edge. I could step back and observe internally: *'Right, you have just reacted quite strongly to something there,'* and then begin to process why that might be.

Whereas before I was focused on asking, 'why can't they just listen to me?' I can now go within and ask of myself: *'What am I not getting here? What am I not doing or seeing?'*

In choosing to 'do life' I made the choice that in every interaction with another person I would make the assumption and hold the intention that actually the other person means well for me, or that they're going to serve or help in some ways. So, for me, by going through all this I faced the question *'Are you doing life or is life doing you?'*

I now describe myself as being awake or awakening whereas before I know that I was just on autopilot and I was doing what other people wanted. At 37 and a half years, statistically, I knew that I was potentially at the mid-point in my life. That realisation alone was very freeing; the realisation of any milestone in life allows the history to be in the past and the future to be a mystery. It was time to be intentional about my own life.

Choose to find your passion

As I came through this dark period, I made a choice to find my passion, my 'fire in the belly'. That started with a decision to say 'yes' - to try things and to assume that people had positive intentions and that they mean well, (unless they proved otherwise).

It hasn't been easy to change my way of thinking. And believe me I'm far from perfect but, I'm enjoying the process. I have been on a journey of learning part of which has taken me from not reading to reading or listening to many of the greatest books in personal development and spiritual awakening. Everything brought me back to love and burning desire. It was time to find my passion. I believe synchronicity or fate stepped in.

I started really asking the question *what makes people tick, what makes some people jump out of bed and change the world and others turn over the TV?*

If I could find out what makes some people tick then I figured that I could put that into a book and share their stories with others, like me, who may be curious or at a turning point in their lives. When I asked people I found our conversations were longer, deeper, more emotional and more impactful. It got to the point where there was more content than needed and as many more questions as those we had found answers to. One thing became very clear to me the greatest learning was in the journey – we couldn't ignore the journey and the steps that had had to happen in order for the moment of awareness, the moment of decision or for their reason why to become clear and non-negotiable.

At that point I had discussions with 20 people to establish what fire in the belly was and had a complex picture of ideas and solutions and we had discussions with a book editor about how we could funnel all these ideas and lessons from all these different people into a coherent text but *how could sharing 10% of their life story give readers a full understanding? What would be lost in the edit?*

It was at this point I believe that fate or synchronicity stepped in. I have been a property investor for over 20 years. In May 2019 I planned to attend a property workshop, due to flight times I had to fly a day earlier and as a result I was invited to attend a podcasting workshop that was running. At the time it just seemed like an interesting thing to do. Within minutes of being in the workshop I had my credit card ready, I realised this was the answer, the way to share 'Fire In The Belly' stories. I knew the question wasn't was I going to do this but how much was it going to cost.

The Fire In The Belly project and podcast was born, a way to effectively communicate and share people's life journey's without cherry picking through all the highs and ignoring all the lows. It is often in the most painful moments that we have the greatest lessons but it's also at those painful points that we are most vulnerable and not always somebody that we want to share. The guests on the show have often been amazingly reflective and generous with their insights and life lessons in a positive way for others to learn from or find recognition within.

The 'Fire In The Belly' podcast went live 9 months later in February 2020 with 50 interviews ready to roll out. We released 20 episodes on the day of launch and have been trying to play catch up ever since. The show has for many guests actually become the by-product of a great conversation, because for many in being given the opportunity to talk, reflect and be heard it has given them a glimpse of their true selves at this point and a birds-eye view of their life so far; the patterns that they have taken on whilst also talking about what their future could hold. That unencumbered view and sense of possibility has, guests say, led to an 'unlocking' and once you get a taste from the elixir of the fountain of 'what could be' you can't undo it or unsee it.

Hearing others through the Fire in the Belly podcast has helped to deepen my understanding of other people and their points of view. I've talked to people who are, or have been, suicidal. I've talked to people who have deep religious beliefs. I've talked to people who have what would be perceived by many as very 'far out' beliefs. I might not agree with the views of everyone I interview, and I might not be able to imagine myself in their shoes, but my role is to listen. I have found that when I provide people with the space and time to explain things to me, in an open way, I might at least understand their point of view and how they benefit from that point of view. At a minimum, through the interview process, I aim to have given them the gift of being heard.

I love that I can dig deep and understand what drives people: different religions, different books, and different ways of living, why someone loves doing that - or doing this. If a guest can explain their point of view and help me understand, then actually quite often some of their passion rubs off on me and I start to feel that passion too.

This is my Fire in the Belly and I intend to keep asking, *'why and what if?'*

To hear and be heard. Listen to your inner genius, let your inner true self come out and roar.

Find and listen
to your inner genius!

20 things to get you
started...

Become OBSESSED to find and listen to the genius that lies within you!

You may not know what your 'Fire In The Belly' is yet … so until you do, here's a list of things to get you started.

'The Genius In you'- inspired by: Think and Grow Rich by Napoleon Hill

1. Your burning desire can simply be to DECIDE to do more, be more and have more! Don't use the excuse that you haven't found your 'why' yet! You are your why! Get off your backside and decide to make the change and your passion, why or purpose will show up.

2. If you don't yet love yourself enough to want to change, then do it for those around you that need you. It's your duty as a human to be of service and to help and inspire others.

3. Learn how to quit and quit doing the things you know are not serving you! If it's not helping you to grow, then it's holding you back.

4. Understand that everyone is on a journey and we're all in different places. Your right may be someone else's wrong. Opinions are like bums, we all have them, but that doesn't mean we should shove them in someone else's face!

5. Call yourself out - did you try your best?

6. Everyone that has a beating heart and breathes air has gifts, potential and fire in their belly! You simply need to give your gifts a chance to grow and come out. Make the decision to grow and evolve.

7. Doing nothing is impossible! Your body, brain and spirit never stop. Time is passing, your body is getting older and inflation is eroding your money. Your car, television and clothes are liabilities and losing value all the time.

8. When you think you're done.... do 5 more things.

9. Accept that 99.999% of words, concepts, thoughts etc. have all happened before. You don't have to have an original idea, you just need to present, reflect or use it in your own way. This is what is unique, and this is as a result of your experiences, ideas and passions - and the way you view them.

10. You're a long time dead ☠. Life is not a dress rehearsal, so at what point are you going to realise that we need to be obsessed with living. What are you waiting for?

11. Learn how you learn.

12. Know you are always capable of more!

13. Every 'problem' you have, is a mindset problem...

Get over yourself! We're all perfectly imperfect.

16. Everyone can teach you something!

17. Try to accept that everyone is fundamentally good.

18. When judging and criticising others, ask yourself, 'what part of what that other person is doing, do you not like about yourself?'

19. Help yourself as much as you help others!

20. Money is just paper, plastic and metal and is neither good nor bad. Money takes the form of the hand it's in.

21. LISTEN. Really listen!!

Chapter Two

Star Trek dragging the Universe behind it

'When you're pushing to do something, you have only got so much willpower.
But when you're pulled, when there's something larger than yourself that you're here to serve and that you believe you're made for, that brings energy.'

- **Tony Robbins**

When someone is pushing to achieve a goal it is often based on getting away from pain and their willpower will often weaken as they progress. Whereas a desire or want-based goal in line with our values and fire in the belly will strengthen as we progress and lead us to feel inspired and pulled towards it.

When we think about trying to listen to our inner genius it may feel like we are the Star Trek Enterprise dragging the universe behind us. When we ask for more and have come to the point of knowing or believing that great things are possible for us, we undertake to do any action that moves us towards that goal and will soon notice that events and opportunities come into our zone of genius. However when we start off on this journey - to be more, do more and have more - most of us will have a lifetime of habits, experiences, results and baggage to step away from to allow us to think and act differently. The decision to change and try something different requires a lot of strength and passion and belief in yourself in order to stretch and break the bonds that can hold you in the past.   At the point that we really hear ourselves we begin to feel inspired and motivated like we are being pulled into a frictionless environment.

There is a tremendous amount of energy and momentum needed to get a rocket ship from earth into space however once in a frictionless environment that same energy could take it to far, far away galaxies.

The power of being heard is in the building of relationships and connection with others and our inner self. Connection is defined in the Oxford dictionary as 'a relationship in which a person or thing is linked or associated with something else.' Positive connections provide a means for the transfer of thoughts, wants, needs and values. These words or communicated ideas carry a level of energy that allow the transfer of information and messages to convey what we need and what we want. It is impossible for any of us to hear the exact meaning being conveyed by the speaker because we will filter the information through our own understanding and experiences.

Social Media

It is in being heard by another that we feel most connection and the more we listen to someone the more they will feel that we 'get them.' This connection is like a strong bond often described as the prized relationships with a best friend, confidante, mentor, counsellor or listening buddy. That person you would meet for a 'chinwag' or to talk through an opportunity in our lives. The more that you spend time together the stronger that connection becomes.

On social media we might have 5 or 500 or 5,000 connections. This type of connection can be either social or professional. In fact, part of the appeal of social media marketing is to have a great number of connections in order to feel wanted, needed and seen. The endorphin hit of the 'like', the ego boost of the 'thumbs up' or 'heart' symbol, the rush of serotonin on the comment and feedback. In terms of life and business this often works for people on a number of levels.

However, when we think about being truly heard in a way that can enrich our lives, here are some questions to consider regarding your connections:

Do you know everyone that you are connected to on social media?

Do you have the same connection with each friend or follower?

How much quality of connection do you have with each person really?

If you were to take time to listen and get to know somebody really well, know their story, know their passions then would this be a more valued connection?

Do you know people in your life that you feel better, more inspired and energised after having spoken with them?

In a connected relationship there is support, a desire to help, respect and an aim to inspire each other to do more, have more and be more. It is a positive connection that gives off positive energy.

If we have a problem or a need to vent, we know the certain people who will listen and can give sound advice. We usually know and can readily name the people we have a positive connection with, when we meet up with them we feel inspired, we feel a warm glow and we may use wording such as; 'lovely to see you,' and 'it's great to hear your voice,' or 'it has been too long.' Often it is because of the history and trust built up over time in the connection that the bond is easily re-ignited.

When we feel heard in a new connection people will say things like, 'I feel like we have been friends all our lives,' or 'I feel like I've known you forever.'

It can be almost disconcerting when someone knows us so well or when we feel that another person really 'gets us' - there can be a level of vulnerability step in because another human being can readily see what we really think, they can hear what we really mean and know how we really feel.

This feeling that they 'get us' normally increases the feeling of being listened to. This is because if someone is mirroring our values, matching our patterns, moods or body language it will feel familiar and can stimulate or simulate a connection.

It is important to be mindful of the difference here as people can use this mirroring subconsciously or deliberately, so that it may or may not be genuine. But because the person reacted in a way that's similar to the way we would have reacted, it can create a feeling and understanding that we are like-minded people.

The subconscious mind is literal and accepts information as fact so this mirroring and simulated connection will feel genuine and appeal to us. Similarly, if the pattern or mirroring feels fake in any way it might cause us to consciously or (perhaps more often) subconsciously reject the relationship or connection.

When we listen to what another person is saying and it rings true, it resonates with us and the connection is strengthened; it's a positive connection.

LIKE RECOGNISES AND ATTRACTS LIKE

In contrast to the positive connections we can make, we might also encounter what I describe as 'mood Hoovers.' People for whom normal and sense of knowing that they are alive is in confirming the glass half-empty mindset or experience of the world – people who currently see the worst in all the best situations and seek out fear, doubt, anxiety and failure. This is their perceived normal and self-defence mechanism. There is a level of consciousness in the connections that we make. One can meet somebody and listening to them can make us feel drained. We feel that we have just had a bit of our life force sucked out of us. That is a negative connection that is somebody with whom the energy is going one way or where we are on different levels of consciousness and there is a real experience of disconnection.

POOR ME GLASSES

WHAT'S YOUR VIEW OF THE WORLD

At the other end of the spectrum there are people who have achieved a lot, have high aspirations for themselves and often have a lot of positive experiences to share. When we meet these people, depending on our own mindset, we might believe that they are more successful than us and feel that we are not on a level playing field with them. This might be because we have had some similar experiences, but we may see them as doing what we haven't and believe that they are more qualified or more connected. We often just feel that we like them, that they would be fun to spend time with and are the type of person we aspire to be, or be with. It's like that famous James Bond quote – 'Women want to be with him, men want to be him.'

WOMEN WANT TO BE WITH HIM,
MEN WANT TO BE HIM

We want to spend time listening to them and, in the case of a celebrity or someone that we don't know personally, we may even feel that they are talking directly to us. Often the opportunity to hear people with this 'star power' is in group settings and when they are speaking to us, it is not a two way conversation. The audience is in receiving mode and they are telling us what they want us to hear. They are sharing their story and are focussed on forming a connection with the audience; they make us feel connected. Even in a room of 10,000 people that's the power of somebody who is able to project their passion.

The people that we want to listen to and connect with give us the best opportunity to find out essential information about how we might live our lives. If we can tap into the way we listen to these people, it will help us listen and connect better with all the people we want to connect with most in our lives. Public speaking is all about your audience as I have learned and share in the following story:

'I have learned that there is a skill in terms of public speaking, of going beyond the illusions that public speaking is about me, about the speaker. I've found in the past that when people said, can you come and give us a 20 minute talk about your journey? I would have taken that at face value initially and it was international mentor Pat Slattery who said to me – 'you do realise this is not about you, don't you?'

I understood that I am being asked for my story but I have learned that really only the first slide or the first two slides or the first two minutes can be about who I am, what I am. After that, people want to hear and connect with what is within my message for them. We connect with messages and experiences that we can resonate with or alternatively when we don't, we will discard them and we see people quickly stop listening.

I want to share my story or message in a way that allows others to hear but also allows them to paint their own picture. I try to hold space so that I am being listened to as I want to feel that we're connecting.

We can be inspired by somebody that we may never meet yet in a split second that one moment of inspiration is enough to change how we feel or make a difference in our lives.'

- Author

Connection

It doesn't take a lifetime for a connection, it can be made in the blink of an eye, and it can just be a moment. It is something that politicians are generally quite good at. Former American President Bill Clinton has been recognised for his ability to get a connection with people whether meeting foreign dignitaries or the average man in the street due to his high levels of charisma.

When we see people who have an ultimate belief in themselves and an alignment in what they believe in, what they believe they are capable of and what they are driven to inspire in those around them then they will be able to connect with people whether they are a politician, a preacher, a leader or an influencer. It's a confidence, energy and strength of conviction that can all be wrapped up under the umbrella of charisma.

Listening is not always via the two lumps on the side of your head. It's listening in terms of how you feel, that feeling in your gut and that's the most powerful form. Connecting and listening are integrally linked.

When we see people who are depressed, they will often isolate themselves and hold back their feelings. To self-isolate or be isolated is one of the most inhuman things we can do to ourselves or others. It is used as a form of punishment, such as telling a child to go to their room; or as a form of bullying to isolate someone from the crowd or group. On the more extreme end, solitary confinement has long been used as a form of punishment and torture.

The COVID-19 pandemic in 2020/21 forced entire swathes of people across the globe into a form of isolation. Forced isolation and voluntary isolation are very different. In voluntary isolation one is choosing to be alone and there is usually the option to come back and join the crowd when ready. In a forced isolation as directed by the government and medical professionals during the global pandemic, people did not choose isolation but were directed and required to stay isolated until told otherwise by an external body.

Fundamentally it's built into us; people want to connect to others. Even as very young children we may not understand the words yet *per se* but we can feel connection, we can hear the warmth, care and love in a caregiver's tone. I believe that finding and surrounding ourselves with people that can and will hear us is the critical first step to hearing the genius within us. If we aren't heard for one reason or another for a long period of time, when we do eventually get the opportunity to speak, it can come out as 'verbal diarrhoea'. Our words and thoughts have been dammed up, and eventually get to the point of overflow.

When we find a great connection and can balance the scales so that we are both listening and being listened to – how often have you said; *'listen, enough about me tell me about you? Tell me what's going on and what's happening here for you.'* And that's permission. As the would-be listener we are thanking the other for the time that they have spent listening and taking the time for us.

Listening to your inner genius and the power of being listened to is on a deep, deep level. We need someone to hear us, to listen to what we are saying. When people think of connection many will resonate back to a family, a home, a point of connection and they bring all these memories reinforcing those connections. It can be super positive. With some family connections the old saying; 'blood is thicker than water,' rings true because we're always going to be connected. We have no choice about that but we can choose if it's going to be positive or negative. These connections to family and friends can also be double-edged as the following experience related on the Fire In The Belly Show illustrates where the host is talking about connection with old friends:

'That's where I feel like I'm most like myself or, you know, people say that when I meet up with old friends, funnily enough, I become like how I used to be as well. That for me is because we are meeting up to reconnect and specifically hear from one another. I want to know what they have been doing – how their lives are going and they're listening to me too, which can be both positive and can be negative. Meeting old friends can bring up old wounds or we can find that we run old patterns or the way we used to be, which can serve to a point, but vice versa, it might be actually they haven't heard who you are now. You know, how many people say, 'my friends have no idea what I do now.'

Is that a healthy connection? A healthy connection is one that is mutually beneficial for both parties, and whilst there may be times of uneven bias on the whole it evens out for you both.'

In our friends and family connections some people will listen and may even be very good listeners, but many of us will choose to formalise listening and being listened to by counsellors, mentors, coaches and all those sort of people as well. We can formalise being heard whereby we are paying someone to listen, to really listen.

You can check that you're being listened to

Hosting a show like Fire in the Belly and hearing the life stories of some 400 people in its first year I am now very aware of a number of things that people will do to show that they are listening and unintentionally or subconsciously will use a number of techniques on the show to show guests that they are being heard in some of the two following key ways:

1. Response signals – we often need someone to overtly recognise us which can be affirmative language like okay or I see etc. Body language can show as raised eyebrows, a nod or shake of the head, a smile or grimace etc. You can tell by facial expression or by the tone that there is a connection and we're subconsciously picking this up all the time.

2. Response seeking - If we are unsure that we are being heard or understood we will often seek a response before we continue and seek to clarify if we are being listened to by asking questions like; *'do you know what I mean? Do you understand what I am saying?'*

We will often question to know if the listener has got us at all, we intuitively sense check all the time in terms of are they listening, what is the connection here? Am I on the right page?

A look can convey a thousand words or a situation may evoke a memory that we share with someone, it happens with siblings all the time. The connection is there because they have got history and they value each other. It can also bring up feelings of vulnerability when someone knows us that deeply. If we are not ready to share, we may actually isolate ourselves from the people that we love most – we're not ready to share yet, or not ready to be around them because we feel vulnerable. We can be in the proverbial washing machine trying to process our own emotions, thoughts and feelings, unable to hear or be heard.

In a strong enough connection, we are able to share (and ultimately we might overshare), but that is because we feel safe enough. Whereas if it's a connection we're maybe not ready for, it may be difficult – it may get emotional or even out of control - we may hear people say; 'I can't do this right now.' If levels of consciousness are not aligned it may be that what we are hearing is not making sense to us. This is how connections may be broken whereby people will quite literally run away; it could be from a problem or a solution - it can be for positive or negative reasons both of which result in a broken connection.

Now consider, who has listened to you?

We will often know the people who really listen to us. Again the most significant tell-tale is when we just feel great around someone or we love meeting up with them. Generally, that happens only with somebody that has listened to us and with whome we have had a broadly equal share of information and connection in listening to each other. Make a note of your 2-3 top listeners. Consider the questions below:

Who do you know is a great listener?

Can you see how they listen?

How do you feel when you are with a great listener?

Listening to self

Listening to ourselves, that little voice and narrator inside our head is essential. On the Fire In The Belly show we ask people to talk about the Junior version of them. Now, typically humans are in their most curious and innocent form up to seven years of age. or some say, like Dr Gabor Maté, up to three years of age.

Consider who are you today versus who you truly are (or at least were), that Junior version. In the experience of many guests and myself as host we find that as we start to consider this it is as if the universe conspires with us to remember. No connection or goal is worth sacrificing or bending our own values, needs, wants and beliefs for.

Mid-life opportunity

And then funnily enough, it is often at the point where we are actually most unlike ourselves - for many, including myself, that was a point of midlife crisis reframed in that it provided a midlife opportunity. It is a common occurrence that people come to a midlife opportunity, when we get far enough along in our lives only to arrive at a point where we feel lost, we don't know what we are doing and for maybe the first time - we know that we don't know what we are doing.

People often decide to isolate, we either go through depression or something that actually allows us to start cutting off because there's too much noise and consideration of what everyone else wants, what you want, what he wants - yet we don't know what we want anymore. We often recognise and don't like people who are trying to fit a persona rather than being their authentic self, it can make us very uncomfortable. Ultimately in listening to ourselves in order to become more aware of our own values, needs, wants and beliefs we realise that we don't want anybody to have to change to meet what they think our expectations are. It often affects us in a negative way, even though the other may think that they are doing it for us. And vice versa we can come to accept that we are doing no-one else a favour by changing ourselves to meet what we think someone else expects,

Passcode

It's a bit like the beauty of a bank card and we all have four digit passcodes in the United Kingdom. A population of some 60 million people yet four digits is enough; we all work to the same system using our card and the four digit code if we want to buy something. It can be the same with people. We may find that there is a passcode to connect to certain people however if we try to change the passcode and we try to change that person and we cannot know the impact on them. The best way we can serve another is to truly listen to them, giving them space to be heard with the objective to do it without judgement. If we come back to the passcode, if we enter a different digit on our pin code then we are not getting the money, we are not getting the connection.

There is a common quote that many people resonate with that is often attributed to Einstein;

'Everybody is a genius. But if you judge a fish by its ability to climb a tree, it will live its whole life believing that it is stupid.'

Mid-Life Questions for us all to consider

Throughout the Fire in the Belly series the questions that people bring up again and again, including those who have experienced a midlife opportunity are;

Does this actually do it for me?

Just because I'm good at it - do I want to keep doing it?

Do I love what I am about to do?

If money and time was no object, what would I do?

The Bucket List Exercise

Also known as the Love List! On the show we often come back to the bucket list which is a beautiful way of starting to identify your goals and your dreams. We are asking you to reconsider the bucket list, to let go of any association with death or 'do before you die' timeframes. A bucket-list is your love-list for the next 5-10 years, just far enough out that it's not going to bring any tension or stress in terms of the ego coming back in and trying to say, you can't do this, you can't do that. The things that people put on their bucket list is so telling; 'I'd love to work with kids,' or 'I would love to go paddle boarding in the Caribbean.'

What do you want to be, do and have? Write it down.

Your Bucket List

The time is now – write your 50 things to be, do and have over the next 5-10 years.

Whatever it is, from the mundane to the mysterious, if you want it – write it!

1.	2.
3.	4.
5.	6.
7.	8.
9.	10.
11.	12.
13.	14.
15.	16.
17.	18.
19.	20.
21.	22.
23.	24.
25.	26.

27.	28.
29.	30.
31.	32.
33.	34.
35.	36.
37.	38.
39.	40.
41.	42.
43.	44.
45.	46.
47.	48.
49.	50.

Bucket List - 50 things to be, do and have!

Your F*%k It List

What do you NOT want to be, do and have? Write it down and let it go...

1.	2.
3.	4.
5.	6.
7.	8.
9.	10.
11.	12.
13.	14.
15.	16.
17.	18.
19.	20.
21.	22.
23.	24.
25.	26.

27.	28.
29.	30.
31.	32.
33.	34.
35.	36.
37.	38.
39.	40.
41.	42.
43.	44.
45.	46.
47.	48.
49.	50.

F*%k It List - 50 things you don't need to experience! Ever (or ever again)

Chapter Three

The 8 Levels of Consciousness Model

'It is in questioning ourselves and in actively listening that the answers may come.'

In listening to some 400 guests over 1,000 hours or 60,000 minutes in the first year of the Fire In The Belly show two things became clear - the importance of clarity and the impact of our levels of consciousness and awareness in how we will frame, accept or learn from our experiences.

Through the Fire in the Belly project a new model to explain consciousness has evolved from what we have heard from guest experiences shared on the show – it is called The 8 Levels of Consciousness Model.

This model has been developed as a way to clarify and explain how guests have experienced shifts in their levels of consciousness and ultimately what we have heard them share about how they have benefitted from insights, shifts and new understandings to improve their life, deepen connections or find peace of mind and happiness.

This model is designed to be practical and show how we can shift our level of consciousness through our thinking.

But first a story...

For the Author the point of great overwhelm was one where he was unconscious and focussed on the external self, Level 8 in the The 8 Levels of Consciousness model, as shared below;

'For me at that time, at 37 and a half, the noise in my head was just flooded. I would be having this conversation, myself sitting here on my left shoulder another on my right. My inner language was brutal. It was saying things like; 'you know, you could try to change, but let's not, I know you, you tried that in the past and you failed.'

Living unconsciously eventually came to a breaking point;

'And I had to change. I didn't do that consciously at the start. I'm not going to take the credit for it. Maybe it was all subconscious in terms of what manifested for me - depression, isolation, losing a tooth and feelings of stress. I still have a missing tooth there. All the stress had built up in me until my body started actually getting rid of pieces of itself as in my tooth. It is a bit of a metaphor in some ways, but also it's a stark reminder to me that my body will actually take over here, and I don't take care of the bus, bits of it will fall off. I was so far from my values and true self that I began to feel that I didn't know what was real. I started to question - what level of the Matrix am I on? And I hear this really regularly on the Fire in the Belly Show. It is a common experience for so many of us, albeit at different times or ages.'

At the point of great overwhelm, people will experience it and react differently but they will all be operating on one of The 8 Levels of Consciousness. This is important because understanding which level we may be operating at allows us to make changes. In order to be heard to be rich, this is critical and something that we can all take steps to do and work on. It is a tangible, practical way of thinking that can help us to unlock the inner genius inside each one of us.

The 8 Levels of consciousness model addresses the experience people have of finding themselves at a point where they are not in line with their true values and true selves.

When our body is in a critical state physically, it will go into a coma to heal. I believe it is the same with our minds: if the noise becomes too much and we stop being able to hear then we may best benefit from silence. This allows the mind to be quiet as we question what changes we can make in our life in order to reach the goals and successes that we want.

We need to accept that we need to learn a few things, learn how to do better self-repairs, and ultimately go on a journey of self-discovery so that we can identify what works best for us and find that fire, the passion and become the mightiest version of ourselves.

If you consider that humans are naturally motivated by avoiding fear, it can help you to understand the best methods of motivating ourselves. I believe most humans are 80% fear driven and 20% pleasure driven. If we know this, we can start to define our goals based on what will give us pleasure. Pleasure-based goals are forward and future based so they get stronger with progress and through time. Fear-based goals however (lack, fear, loss etc based) lose their momentum as progress is achieved so in turn become less effective and the chance of failure rises.

What if you accepted your fears as your positive motivation to create your pleasure? And used your pleasure motivations to discover and overcome your fears and inspire an even greater evolutionary change?

CONFUSION AND COURAGE

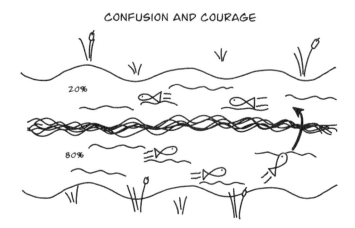

Which bus are you on?

An analogy that is often used is the idea of people as their own bus, the fact is that we are each the drivers in our own lives. If our lives are a bus we must consider which one we are on.

The first bus is moving along the motorway at a steady and efficient 56mph, it does not stop but moves consistently forward. The pace is measured and the passengers and driver look happy. It stops for fuel, it may take detours but it is steadily moving in the direction of its destination.

The second bus starts off fast at 90mph along the same motorway, the fuel is being used up quickly and the passengers and driver look a little tense. There are parts falling off the bus, it must frequently stop for fuel and other drivers are blasting their horns. Its progress is very much stop – start.

Be the first bus.

'True communication is communion – the realisation of oneness, which is love.'

-   **Eckhart Tolle**

Levels of Awareness

In order to prepare for the 8 Levels of Consciousness Model it may be useful to consider your level of awareness, or self-awareness. Self-awareness theory is based on the idea that you are not your thoughts, but the entity observing your thoughts; you are the thinker, separate and apart from your thoughts. (Duval & Wicklund, 1972)

Levels of awareness are often talked about on the show and the following illustration is a simple method to show the different levels of awareness and how we may experience them in terms of how we feel and the type of energy or productivity level that we may experience in each state.

LEVEL OF AWARENESS

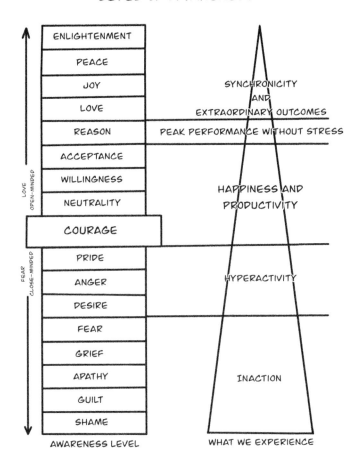

Can we change our level of awareness and emotions?

Let's consider the 5 stages of grief model which is used to reflect how people cope with illness and dying and further how their family and friends will also often go through a similar process. It illustrates that one can move through different emotions and may experience these cyclically to eventually come to a state or stage of acceptance through changes in our levels of awareness. The observance of these emotions and understanding of them within a grief model may help people to better cope through knowledge and acceptance that their feelings will change over time.

5 STAGES OF GRIEF

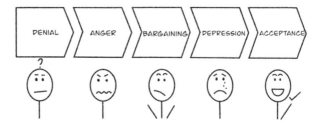

Knowing?

In dictionary.com, *knowing* is defined as; 'having knowledge or information; intelligent, shrewd, sharp, or astute. Conscious; intentional; deliberate.'

When it comes to finding our fire and passion, we do not always know with any certainty or clarity exactly what it is we desire. Knowing in itself requires experience, evidence under decision, thought and mindset, based on our previous experiences. Within every human being is a subconscious mechanism that allows our bodies to function, to learn from experiences, and form a view of the world. When we complete a task successfully, we can say that we know that it was successful because we have seen it. When we have previous experiences open in our minds we can follow logic to say that we know what will happen as we have the same or a similar comparable experience.

Knowing is an invisible force, it's a combination of years of experience, opinions, ideas, failures and successes. But what we know has a limit in itself as can be demonstrated in the four quadrants of knowing:

1. **Knowing that you know.** When you have experience, facts, confirmation that you know something is true.
2. **Knowing that you don't know.** When you are aware that you lack the necessary knowledge, skills or experience to know if something is true or factual.
3. **Don't know that you know.** When something is known but you have not questioned it or become aware of something within your experience or knowledge.
4. **Don't know what you don't know.** When something is outside of your experience or you have not become aware of a fact, issue

or area of life before. Alternatively it may be that you think you know something but you are not factually correct in your thinking on a subject.

The power, opportunity and potential lies in the fourth quadrant but the risk of the ego, limiting beliefs and self-talk originate in quadrants 1 and 2.

We cannot empower somebody else, the same as we cannot lead a horse to water and force it to drink. Only we can decide what we want, what we are capable of, what we are willing to sacrifice, what our deepest desires, visions and expectations are. Empowerment is a state of mind. We step into an empowered state when we focus our mind and physical actions on achieving specific goals and or tasks that align with our mission and vision for our lives. When we know it is possible to achieve a goal, it's no longer a case of whether it can be achieved, but simply a question of what is required to achieve it and if we are willing to spend the required time, energy and perseverance to make it happen.

There is an expression 'to know and not do is really not to know,'- outlined by Stephen R Covey in The 7 Habits of Highly Effective People. This is a great example of modern-day life; we have excess knowledge and opportunity but still we don't empower ourselves or take the appropriate action.

The invisible force of knowing is ultimately there to keep us safe but the ability to stand aside and test our knowledge, awareness and beliefs, is where the concept of change and empowerment takes place. As humans we often know what we want but in a greater way we more often know what we don't want. We know the difference between right and wrong, positive and negative, up and down, failure and success, but this is indeed subject to our belief mechanism and values.

There is a concept that says everything you need to know is already within you, but the key part is to remember and apply that knowledge, which also links back to the power of knowing. Our subconscious and superconscious mind - that level of consciousness that sees beyond material reality - has more capability and ability to judge, measure, evaluate, project and decide than humans will ever be able to realise or measure in a scientific way. Therefore, acceptance of subconscious and superconscious knowing is one of the hardest things to accept because it relies on an element of blind faith.

The ability to trust and believe and have faith in the unknown is not a new principle because is not every religion and spiritual belief in the universe based on an element of faith and alignment?

It is to let go of expectations that may have been piling up since childhood; how many beliefs, attitudes, adopted values and expectations of others are weighing you down?

Inside every one of us is a voice and often several voices. There is the voice of our inner critic, there is the voice of our better selves, but fundamentally there is also our true voice which comes from our inner genius and is there to speak to us and guide us – but only if we let it. Voices and noises within our heads are all influenced by those around us, social media, world events, our families, and feedback on our health, wealth and expectation of success.

One of the most powerful concepts can be the acceptance to say that I know that I do not know but I am willing and open to finding out. Therefore, it is critical for us to have the space, peace of mind, capacity and willingness to listen to what we really want and know without fear of retribution, judgement, or failure. This can be the point of change whereby we step out of the firing line.

POINT OF CHANGE

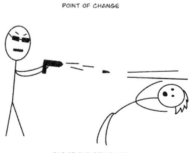

OUT OF THE FIRING LINE

'Knowing is not enough; we must apply.

Willing is not enough; we must do.'

— Johann Wolfgang von Goethe

How many ways do you refer to yourself? How many tenses do you use?

Below are some common ways that we address the different personas or aspects within ourselves. When you start a sentence you may say; 'I like to think of the future.' When talking about 'my future' it may be a different part of yourself. When we think about our future the word we is generalised, sometimes you use your name and say; 'Bob what were you thinking?' We may use 'you' when referring to ourselves as in 'why did you do that?' or when we use he/she it is often a third party commentary on the self. The use of different tenses indicates that you are verbally addressing different parts of yourself that may have different ideas, beliefs, aspects or characteristics.

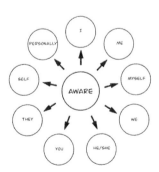

The 8 Levels of Consciousness Model (A.K.A The Russian Doll Vortex Model)

As people there is a secret truth that can change our lives. Our level of consciousness will determine how we show up in the world and directly influence what we experience. There are 8 levels of consciousness and understanding these can help each of us to change our thoughts and actions to achieve success, whatever that means to each of us. To be rich in life is to have our needs, wants, values and beliefs in alignment with who we are and how we show up in the world. To experience love, joy, peace and happiness within and in our connections.

Everything that we want to achieve is within us. We can find and listen to our inner genius by moving through the 8 levels of consciousness - and we are going to show you how. This is practical knowledge that you can accept and use to experience your knowing and see the richness that you were born with.

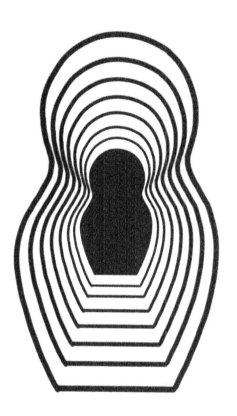

Level 8 – Unconscious

This is a level that all too many are living in, the state of unconsciousness. At this level of consciousness many people are living like a coiled spring, locked down and tense in the lowest state of thinking and vision. In this state we are self-focussed, and may be living in a state of fear, doubt and disbelief.

Like the Tinman in the Wizard of Oz people may speak of feeling empty inside and are looking without rather than within for fulfilment, love, peace and happiness.

First Dimension - Thinking that everything is up to us. Everything is about getting through life, that something just is and the belief that things are happening to us.

It's You versus the World. You are your Ego.

Primal, fear-based, blockages - fear of loud noises and falling.

Don't know what you don't know.

Point of least listening.

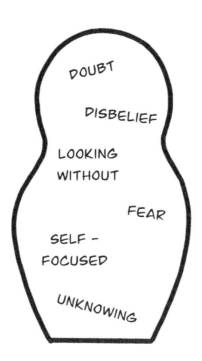

Level 7 - Mid-Conscious

At this point people start to understand that there may be something more to life and begin to free their mind to the potential of a higher purpose. This level is often indicated through a belief in fate or luck.

At this point we may still be looking without and people often ask questions like 'Why is this happening to me? What did I do?'

Second Dimension – People open to the potential that there may be something more to life than ourselves. Vulnerability starts to creep in.

Separation between fact and opinion and possible incongruence – recognising I said this but I did that. People start to seek meaning.

Inner dialogue can be noisy.

Don't know that you know.

Point at which we may start to ask questions and *try* to listen.

Level 6 - Inner-Conscious

This is the start of opening to change and the level at which we first begin to understand that we have choice. Guests talk about how at this level they started to hope that there is more to life. However at this level we may still think, 'when I see it I will believe.'

We may start to ask 'What is the purpose of my life?'

Third Dimension – Seeing – becoming aware that there are three levels to a person; the subconscious, the conscious and the body. Ego-awareness and a new ability to hold two opposing thoughts – to recognise that part of me gets annoyed at that and part of me doesn't mind or that part of me wants to believe yet part of me will believe it when it happens.

(Still) Don't know that you know.

Point of being able to hear.

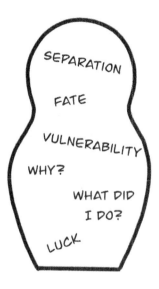

Level 5 – Conscious

This is the point of change, a growing sense that the answers are out there looking for us as we open to the possibility in our lives.

We start to understand and believe that there is more to life and there is a higher purpose at play. We may often think in terms of karma or a growing desire to do good so that good things will happen or a sense that because I did this then that happened.

Fourth Dimension – Point of change; in addition to the subconscious, conscious and body we accept the growing awareness that we can make a choice at all times within our lives. Experiences of déjà vu. Awareness of self and that we can change our state and deliberately alter or adjust our moods. Awareness of universal energy.

Knowing that you don't know.

Point of starting to go within to listen to your inner genius.

Level 4 - Sub-Conscious

This is the point of acceptance. At this point we may choose to apply blind faith in life. Guests talk about having a sense of wonderment and amazement. At this level we begin to gain insights into our true values, needs, wants, beliefs and experiences.

Many people will talk of a sense of waking up or awakening and starting to see changes in their lives. We may experience a growing sense that we have constructed our lives with the programmes that we choose to run. An understanding that up to this point we may have been asking the wrong questions.

Fifth Dimension – Acceptance – a growing sense that whatever it is, it is possible. Suddenly becoming aware that we are definitely a small fish in a huge pond and not the reverse. The understanding of self as a minnow in the ocean of life which can be amazing and frightening at the same time.

Apart thinking – we may still have a belief that we are separate; a sense of me *and* the universe.

(Still) Knowing that you don't know.

Point of awakening and ability to actively hear ourselves and others.

Level 3 - Super Sub-conscious

Point of serenity and harmony with ourselves, our lives and the world around us. This is the Soul level. At this point we can often feel that we are in the real world for the first time and guests have talked about experiencing the world in a new way. This is the point of freedom and the level of consciousness at which people will let go of all fear, doubt and disbelief.

We may hear people share an understanding or belief that there is no truth – only facts and opinions. We develop an understanding that we have choice and control over our actions.

A sense that nothing is real only that which our mind makes real.

Sixth Dimension – Serenity

Knowing that you know.

Point of fully developed listening and hearing.

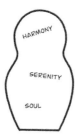

Level 2 - Inner-Genius

This is the 'I am' level of consciousness. The point at which we can bend the universe and become fearless in meeting life.

At this point we move from a growing sense of knowing the path to actually walking the path. Life begins to feel effortless and guests talked about experiencing total trust in the process and their own ability to live and be and do in a world where anything is possible. At this level of consciousness, Inner-Genius, we fully understands that wherever we are in life it is a choice that we are making.

Seventh Dimension — I am. Completeness and wholeness. Trust. Dream state – no awareness of restrictions or boundaries, everything just is, understanding I can do anything.

Enlightenment.

Point of Inner-Genius.

Level 1 – Oneness

This level of consciousness is one of being in a state of Oneness. The 'I.'

The experience at this level is said to be one of universal energy. The knowing and the experience that we are all one level of consciousness.

As I am, so are you, As you are, so am I.

Eighth Dimension – Oneness. We experience universal consciousness and understand that as we raise our level of consciousness we raise the level of consciousness for others. Experience of being one with all that is.

Oneness.

Point of Universal Energy and Oneness.

Point of Universal Energy / Oneness / Source Energy

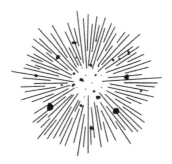

In the film, The Matrix, there is a point when the character Neo becomes aware of all the various levels of consciousness. This would be akin to somebody who is perceived as enlightened, who has reached the level of Oneness.

Being In The Matrix

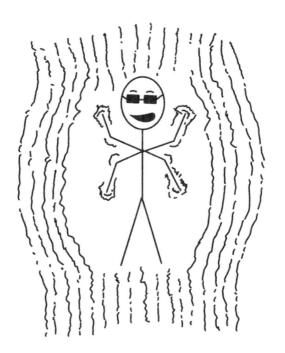

Walking the Path

The 8 Levels of Consciousness Model can be used as a path for life. It is a way of hearing life; the world within us and around us to find richness in all areas of our life through our own level of consciousness – our awareness, beliefs and choices.

When our level of awareness begins to shift, grow and expand through the levels of consciousness we usually find that we fluctuate between levels. For many people it can feel like a shedding or releasing of all their programmes and constructs to find their core-self, core-truth, their own soul character. For others of us it may feel like an expansion, a growth in awareness and knowledge that enables us to be more, do more and have more. We expand our level of consciousness and, in so doing, we can uncoil from any limiting programmes and beliefs that may have made us feel restricted. We can effectively tip the scales from fear and doubt to find new hope.

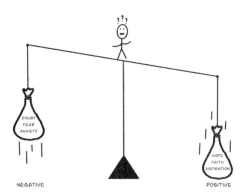

As an engineer by training and profession I think of this process much like the refraction process. Refraction is a process whereby an energy source is deflected from a straight path and passes from one medium or one level to another in which its velocity or speed will become different. As with refraction so it is with moving through the levels of consciousness. Guests on the show have shared that as they moved through the levels of consciousness they experienced both their thinking and timeframes changing and speeding up. This may be thought of in terms of increased clarity and ability to move in the direction of our life goals. People have found that they have achieved success quickly and effortlessly where previously they found closed doors or difficulties.

In the fluctuation stages and as we start to move through the levels of consciousness it can feel frightening, we may question our sanity and the reality around us. If we imagine ourselves as being refracted on our path then we may be able to understand that we are having to adapt quickly to a new medium and speed that we haven't experienced before.

Take time to consider your level of consciousness and how you can open your thinking to new levels of consciousness, to be heard and to listen to your inner genius.

This will be explored further in chapter nine and there is an exercise, The 7 Levels Deep Exercise, that will help you to really explore this further but first let's further unpack some of these concepts.

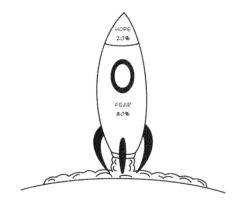

Chapter Four

Fire in the Belly

'Is your inner genius being heard?
Find your fire.'

In starting to hear myself I chose to do and follow what I was hearing and started to discover my fire, my passion and uncover what being the mightiest version of myself would mean for me. I believe that everyone has an inner genius within them that some will unlock. That everyone has a fire in their belly - some people call it their purpose, some their passion and others call it their mission. Let's find yours.

What's your Fire In The Belly?

Listen to your gut instinct and that voice within you. Give yourself space and time and release your expectations as you go within to hear what to be rich would mean for you. There is no right or wrong when it comes to finding the mightiest versions of ourselves. On the Fire In The Belly show there are two essential questions that are regularly asked of guests – I have shared them previously but now it is time for you to answer them.

Take the time and space to go within, you may want to rest beforehand or choose to be in a quiet place.

Sit and take a few deep breaths.

Then ask each question and hear the answer.

Question: What do you really want?

I come back to that question regularly both with myself and with guests because when we strip off everything else; school holidays, life, overdrafts and friends - the conversations with yourself of 'he said, she said, I didn't say, I didn't do this, I did do that!' the only thing that really is what is important to us in order to meet our needs and want and be in alignment with our values.

'What do you really want?' is the question that will enable you to answer and find what does being rich means for you?

Could it mean to deepen your connections, create success, build wealth, and find peace of mind, happiness or whatever else it means for you? What do you really want? Write it down below:

Question: What will you think of just before you die?

On the show when we listen to people who have had near-death experiences, and probably subconsciously I have some understanding of it having hit rock bottom, the near-death experience always seems to mark a before and after in their lives. In her best-selling book, Dying to be Me, Anita Moorjani talks about her near-death experience as one of a feeling of peace and quiet. She shares that at the moment her body was done, shutting down and she felt ready to leave her body - the meat suit if you like - and some people on the show have also talked about that moment, as one when they just let go of everything.

So, what will you think of just before you die? Again, write it down below:

'So, if you think you're this 'meat suit' running around, think again. You're a spiritual being! You're an energy field, operating in a larger energy field.'

- **Rhonda Byrne, The Secret**

Finding your Fire In The Belly can feel like that, like a stark realisation or post adrenaline fatigue where you feel kind of faint. When people do a parachute jump, and quite often it's something they have wanted to do for years, when they hit the ground they often report feeling elation and absolute exhaustion or a moment of silence. Guests report similar feelings when things start to come together for them and they find their why, their passion and ultimately their fire in the belly. For so long we may have wanted this or that and suddenly when we receive it or buy it or create it – we may not know what to do anymore.

It's in that silence, in the asking and hearing the answers that we find clarity. When we can say, 'This is all I focused on. This is all I wanted.'

Ikigai

In Japanese culture there is the concept of Ikigai –part of which is the expectation that finding ones fire in the belly is central to life. In finding this the Japanese believe people will do work because they are passionate about it and fulfilling both their potential and purpose. That is a very positive way of living. A lot of people in the Western world still plan to work until they receive a retirement pot and to follow their passions at that point. Ikigai is the opposite and shows a way of living in the gap in terms of living as who we truly are versus who everyone recognises us as. I will talk more about Ikigai in Chapter Six.

Definitely Yes or Hell No?

When it comes to our fire in the belly there can only be two answers in the flow chart of life. Is it a Definitely Yes or a Hell No?! Get rid of any okay box or idea that people do things because they have to, or they believe they have to or for any of 50 different reasons.

We have to listen to ourselves and answer ourselves honestly - for every question, from the most basic to the most profound, is it a Definitely Yes or a Hell No? If someone asks do you want to go swimming? Hell No. And we realise that it is okay to say No, whereas we might have gone in the past.

Be unreasonable

Two of the most dangerous and over-used terms are good and okay. These are generic catch-all terms used often because we either haven't consolidated our thinking or are feel under social duress to not give an opinion. If you think of a passionate person one of their attractive qualities is their definiteness of purpose and conviction of state. A reoccurring theme at the moment is to fail fast and fail hard which dovetails with the mantra of everything has a purpose and a purpose for everything. If everything you do you do with passion, even when unsure of the outcome or likelihood of success, simply doing it to the best of your ability means you will succeed even when you fail. When exploring a goal or a vision endeavour to do it as quickly and with a 'go all in' attitude. We can learn and evolve en route.

The mantra of fail to plan, plan to fail will sometimes need to be bypassed because the plan and vision may only become clear as momentum and emotion is gained. Often our subconscious patterns and burning desires only become obvious when we start to take action towards our perceived goals and you will notice that certain activities will have a greater emphasis or are completed with greater energy because of a natural in-built or subconscious enthusiasm.

When setting out on a journey that will require passion and focus and dedication it is critical to drop the dead load of items that do not bring you love or joy. On the show and over the past four years I have learned that people experience massive positive shifts when they become totally unreasonable in letting go of the areas that do not serve us and we are not best suited to serve with our skills and passion.

Just think, in life, if you were only to do the things that brought you love and joy how freeing could that be?

It is actually in trying to be reasonable to everything and everyone that ultimately leads to a people pleasing state. When in that state long enough all authority and confirmation solely comes from the feedback of others which means that we no longer have clarity on our own feelings and require the feedback from others to let us know how we feel. When we have become incredibly reasonable, pleasing, mediocre and all drive and ambition has been watered down for the greater good our ambitions will be stepped down to meet with the average of the medium.

What if you chose not to water down your passions and your goals?

What if you stood with unreasonable focus and drive - A drive that would excel you to make and create a whole new life for yourself which in turn would create a remarkable journey for you and those closest to you?

'If it's going to be: It's up to me.'

- **Dr Robert Schuller**

Remember: Put Your Own Oxygen Mask On First

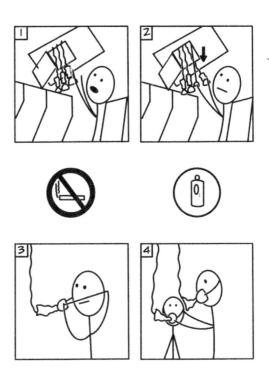

The 12 Principles of Being Unreasonable

Be unreasonable when focussing on your goals.

Be unreasonable when distractions and dilutions come your way.

Be unreasonable when your bad habits want you to stay in bed or that voice in your head says okay is good enough.

Be unreasonable when you have a choice of doing the fun thing or that action that will make your boat go faster.

Be unreasonable when the opinion of others can cloud your soul and distract your vision.

Be unreasonable when those that know you best help you the least.

Be unreasonable when comparing yourself to others – the only true comparison is to who you were yesterday and what your greater self could be doing tomorrow.

Be unreasonable when you are striving for a goal that is to prove a point rather than to achieve greatness, be driven by pleasure not pain.

Be unreasonable when setting your big future goals and vision. Your job is to ask, believe, do and receive.

Be unreasonable when listening to your own story; understand that your truth may not be true at all. What is the truth but a series of compounded stories told often enough and with certainty so that it becomes your truth? Be cautious of assumptions and perhaps a suggested mantra of 'I don't know,' and a willingness to listen is truly empowering.

Be unreasonable when you go to dismiss that little voice in your head or that gut feeling because that may well be the response of your sub-conscious inner genius.

Be unreasonable because death of your physical body is coming.

'I am the master of my fate:

I am the captain of my soul.'

\-   **William Ernest Henley (1849-1903)**

'The most powerful force in the universe is compound interest.'

- **Albert Einstein**

Compound Interest

Many of us have lost a job or faced redundancy or felt depressed at some point in our lives or come to the point where everything was mediocre or okay and all our efforts were being made to be reasonable. For me it was the realisation that life was happening to me rather than through me. The common thought in my head at that time was, *what if?* At that point and as the company folded I found that there was something wrong with the formula that I had been operating. It felt like a jinx in the Matrix, in one scene in the film the audience sees a lady in a red dress walk past amongst people in blacks and greys and the viewer knows that there is something wrong.

At the point of overwhelm take time to ask others and ourselves, *what do you want, what do you want, and what do you really want?*

When I started to ask, the truth was that I didn't know what I wanted, but eventually I heard this sort of whisper - and for me that was the whisper of the subconscious – and the answer was very simple – *'what if you said yes?'*

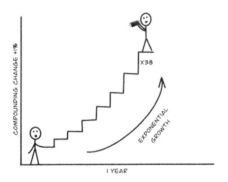

'Small, seemingly insignificant steps completed consistently over time will create a radical difference.'

- **Darren Hardy**

The One Per Cent System

I read The Compound Effect by Darren Hardy and decided to make a one per cent change every day and create a system for myself so for 14.4 minutes - which is 1% of a day - for 14.4 minutes every day I committed to do something a little bit different, to try something new that would be future-generating what I wanted to see in my life.

In this system we dedicate 14.4 minutes to read a book or assign tasks or send five emails.

Tomorrow, another 14.4 minutes and that first 14.4 minutes is still working for us. Repeat it again the next day and in 14.4 minutes send five recommendations or five more emails to people we would you like to connect with or share information with that may benefit them. So the next day in the 14.4 minutes slot, chances are someone from the first 14.4 minutes has started to respond and the work that you assigned to somebody else, well that's continued going as well.

In this way that 1% per day, those 14.4 minutes start to compound so that after a year you can expect a 38 times greater positive change from where you started. *Yes a 38 times positive change.*

Another way to visualise this is to consider it in terms of a monetary investment. If we start by investing an initial balance of £1 in a fund with compound interest of 1% every day then at the end of one year or 365 days the investment value will be £37.78 or some 38 times its original value.

Investment Projection 1% daily compound interest over 365 days:

Initial Balance:	£1.00
Total Days:	365
Total Investment Value:	£37.78
Total Interest/ earnings:	£36.78
Percentage Profit:	3678.3%

*** It is important to note that this same compounding effect can also work in the opposite way. We will 38x our results if we are focusing on 14.4 minutes of positive, future generating activities or building relationships. Make the 1% work for you, ensure you spend it on what you want.

Be Heard or Die

Often when something happens we talk about how a little piece of us has died with something or someone.

The reality is that a little piece of us is dying all the time.

If we are not listening to ourselves, or if someone is not being heard or listened to, in the most extreme cases the consequences can be death. The very core and purpose of what listening organisations like the Samaritans do is in their slogan – 'If you need someone to talk to, we listen. We won't judge or tell you what to do' and 'Whatever you're facing. We're here to listen.'

At Fire In The Belly guests and the team have expressed their gratitude that services like the Samaritans are there for people and it is their message – 'we listen' - that we have found, through 1,000 hours of listening, is the most basic yet fundamental form of showing up and connecting with people.

In writing this book during lockdowns across much of the world in 2020 many social media posts were aimed toward mental health and in particular suicide awareness and the importance of listening. Many posts contained contrast, on one side after a person's death - we wish they'd told us, we wish we'd listened. On the other side, before the suicide perhaps identifying potential cries for help, instead is listed the idea that someone is perhaps seeking attention or complaining or isolating. These are things that as a society and as a people we can learn. That the more we are willing to listen to people and start to understand the very fact that for so many of us we come to that point where we're not able to listen to ourselves, which is terrifying for anyone who has ever experienced it. How frightening the noise can be, not knowing what to do, having to isolate, having to shut down because we feel that there's no choice.

It is at those points that if we are able to listen to ourselves, or we have someone to listen to us then we can find our fire in the belly and a new path will open to us, a path of learning and lessons and growth. In listening and talking we can come to the point of identifying clearly our passion and our reason.

I would like to share this experience with a guest on the show...

Asking the next most obvious question

'On the first 100 episodes of the Fire In The Belly show one of the guests talked openly about periods of suicidal ideation that have repeated and are ongoing in their life. That show will not air as agreed with the guest. As they talked openly about feeling suicidal, as show host I asked the next most obvious question; *'Why don't you kill yourself?'*

And a lot of people on the team said, 'you didn't ask that did you?' Yes, I did, from a place of listening, non-judgement and in seeking understanding and the person accepted the question. The guests response was; 'that is one of the best questions I've ever been asked and the most relevant.'

In that moment, we got down to their reason for living – they changed their tone and body language as their fire in the belly clarified. Their answer? 'Because I have so much to do and there's so much I want to do. And I want to live.'

I would most probably not have asked that question of another guest but I was led by what I felt was right in terms of their language, their response and their energy. And sometimes we need a pattern break.

Sometimes we just need someone to go, *'what are you doing? What do you mean?'*

Painting the picture

One of the first questions on the show is normally how are you today? As long as the answer to that is okay then we are on a journey built up of experiences and lessons and sharing the learning that a guest has gained or achieved.

That old statement, 'mind your own business,' is an important one and that's not to be rude. It's a way to consider how we are minding our own business in terms of the way that we do things or are minding the way we view things. Others opinions, their ideas or any potential for influence on us is none of our business.

We can't apply our beliefs or values to understand another person but what we can do is listen and ask them to paint us a picture, to tell us and speak to us about what their view is. Ironically, in asking them to paint a picture they are then painting it in their own head. Suddenly guests will get this moment of realisation because the show has created that gap and safe space for them to just talk it out and start to process it by removing any outside influences.

Suddenly the guest has a realisation – 'ah, that's what it is.' As the person listening you may still be painting the picture but for them things have been revealed.

On my Dad, David Lonton's gravestone it reads;

'Live life with no regrets'

How?

In listening to over 400 guests I have learned that in order to live the journey with no regrets we need to say yes, to then check how we feel about that and then check the consequences.

In all of this, at the end of the day I've got to feel that it's right for me. I've got to accept me. I've got to love me. I've got to be okay with me. I can't afford the weight of the baggage of everyone else. So my fire in the belly is the Fire In The Belly project. It's helping people. It's seeing people switch on, saying I'd love to do that, this is what I want to do. It's enough of a seed at this time for it to bring hope, to bring faith to people who are able to say I have a reason. I have a why that's not disassociated on to my kids or the person that I love or on to somebody else or how I love.

It is there in the question, *'what do you love to do?'*

If we look at Elon Musk and Space X their mission statement is super clear - they're going to Mars. That's the mission. That's the vision. Do they know how to get to Mars? No, but they're firing off rockets left, right and centre. At Space X they're all clear that they're heading to Mars. With every failure, as record-breaking baseball great Babe Ruth said – 'every strike brings me closer to the next home run,' it's like every ball SpaceX hit, it's closer to the next right one, the next positive one, the next connection and so it all builds and builds and builds and builds. They future pace it by talking only in terms of when we visit Mars, it's already a statement of fact for the project team, it's not a question.

If it's not getting them to Mars it is not happening. When we are on a mission and have a purpose we radiate energy. When I ask people, *what is your fire in the belly?* Their smile is ear to ear, that question has just dug into their core and bypassed their consciousness and as they answer, together we've suddenly gone into the world of the Doctor Seuss's, the world of magical moments and worlds and endless possibilities.

In hearing our fire in the belly we have the power to really shift our lives massively. If we can just listen long enough and objectively enough to ourselves and others so that we go past the point of being okay we can then connect and draw a line across to the passion, the why. We have a reason, it mightn't be the final reason, but it's enough to actually drag us forward and to get positive energy, see potential opportunity and create ideas.

Fake it until you make it?

Do you believe in faking it until you make it? Does acting as if change your future?

I have come to believe that faking it until you make it is a double edged sword, that if you have to force it, it's not meant to be. The concern with this statement is the word fake and the connotation of fakery or not being the real thing. A better term may be:

'Do it until you become it.'

Life is a journey of trying until successful, the old analogy of a baby will try to hundreds of times before it is able to walk. Don't give up.

We are capable of more than we can comprehend in a thousand lifetimes, every single one of us.

I come back to the 1%, what if you started doing 14.4 minutes of extra future building and forward moving stuff every day. It's not just having another chat. It's logging extra time and having an ongoing effect. That's how we see stuff changing - life changing.

'Everyone has an inner genius within them that some will unlock.'

In compounding that 1% every day for a year you not only 38x your outcomes but you start to actually create a vacuum behind you because you've done this, this, this and this. The universe seems to say - because you did that then you saw this opportunity, which has given off energy and encouraged someone else ... and suddenly we are back to Star Trek dragging the Universe behind it. We open a world of possibilities by finding our Fire In The Belly.

How to Be Heard To Be Rich

In All Areas of Your Life

In the previous chapters we have outlined the reasons for, and concepts of, being heard. *What can you do to ensure that you are being heard and hearing others?*

In the following six chapters we will fully explain how to put it into practice and show you the tools and exercises that can take you from feeling stranded or lost at sea to being rich in life; deepen your connections, create success, build wealth, and find joy, love, peace of mind and happiness.

Chapter Five

Create Space

'We all have a quiet voice inside us. We need to create the space and block all outside noise to be able to hear it.'

On the Fire in the Belly show we prepare guests to be heard. Once a guest has confirmed we send them an email and set out that the only aim and intention for the show is to get to hear about them – their journey, their lessons, their successes and their experiences.

This is a rare gift for anyone on this planet. I ask you to reflect now on the following two questions:

1. *When was the last time you were asked to talk only about yourself, just to be you?*

2. *Now, consider when was the last time you felt heard by another?*

These are important questions for us as human beings. On the show one of our key aims is that the guest will be comfortable so firstly we create space in terms of time by asking them to allow up to two hours for their life story talk. This often surprises people initially, especially people in business or media who may be used to preparing soundbites for time limited interviews that have a pre-arranged purpose and a desired outcome. The only aim on the Fire in the Belly show is to allow time and to hear what a guest has to say. Guests are not asked to come prepared apart from considering any subjects or topics that they really don't want to discuss and setting the intention for themselves to share their story in a way that will serve them and others.

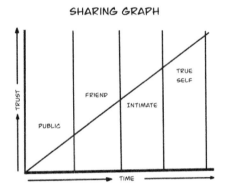

Time to Talk

I ask you, would you be willing to be interviewed for two hours?

We have heard many guests question why they need to allow two hours for an interview, even the concept can immediately take many of us out of our comfort zones. Just consider the space that is being offered – to hear them for two protected hours which ultimately is asking the other person to talk for two hours.

Many are surprised at the resistance that they feel or initially laugh at the idea that they will be talking for over 30 minutes, that seems to be the accepted maximum interview length before guests come onto the Fire in the Belly show.

'Sometimes people just need a damn good listening to!'

- **René Carayol MBE**

The two-hour time request is non-negotiable for the show and once space has been created and we have confirmed that the focus is on hearing from the guest then we look to create safety within that space. In order to do that each guest is reassured that there are no right or wrong answers, just their memories, thoughts and opinions.

JUST BECAUSE YOU ARE RIGHT, DOES
NOT MEAN, I AM WRONG.
YOU JUST HAVEN'T SEEN LIFE FROM MY
SIDE

The fact that the show will be recorded means that they have the opportunity to watch it back and must agree to its being published. We also retain the right to refuse to release an episode of the Fire in the Belly show if we think that it will not serve the guest or the show.

For a variety of reasons around a third of recorded episodes do not get released and the majority of these will be recorded again before being released. The feedback that we hear most from guests is of the positive impact the interview experience has had on them and almost everyone will tell us that it's one of the best conversations they have had in a long time. *What is it that makes them feel it has been a conversation?* As host I have been there to hear them, to ask some questions but mainly just to listen.

From reviewing guest feedback and in post-interview chats some common themes have become clear. Here are the eight Fire In The Belly Top Tips for Creating Space to Be Heard:

Fire In The Belly Top Tips for Creating Space to Be Heard

1. Define and allow lots of time, we allow two hours as it takes the first 20-30 minutes to go beyond conscious and conditioned responses.

2. Agree to spend the time together, whether online or face to face, free from other distractions – e.g. turn off the phone, be home alone, put the dog out.

3. Ask open questions. An open-ended question is a question that cannot be answered with a 'yes' or 'no' response, e.g. *why, what, how questions; why did you say that at the time? What did you learn, if anything? How did you feel about that?*

4. Don't anticipate answers, hear what is being said and respond in the moment.

5. Remember you are there to hear another person that is your only job.

6. This is their story, you may think that you have an opinion, leave it aside before the conversation starts and just hear them out.

7. Use open body language. Consider how you are sitting, do not cross your arms or legs. Make reasonable eye contact and show that you are listening by nodding your head, making sounds to indicate that you are listening.

8. See it as an opportunity to learn and be prepared to change the way that you look at things.

Allowing two hours together in a protected space free from distractions, dogs and other people etc. also results in the space becoming a facilitator, we are creating a bubble - whether we are together in person or online - it works in the same way. In the feedback from guests we have identified two main recurring themes. Firstly, just how much they loved to have that time to talk, and secondly how during the interview they have found that they have formalised their own thoughts on certain things. Sometimes it's in that opportunity of having the space to just talk that we can understand what we ourselves really think.

In terms of understanding the polarity of the space and of the discussion we ask you to consider *are you being bitter or better? In your life story talk are you victim or victor?*

This space on the show is for the victor to reflect on the journey that has happened and perhaps the victim that they may have been at a point. To show how they have chosen a better way or path.

Guilt-free guilty pleasure?

An open question that we are asking guests more and more is *'what's your guilt-free guilty pleasure?'*

We do not set any context at all, it is not a question of guilty in terms of any specific area of their life. Now somebody might turn around and go oh, I really love a certain brand of chocolate – and actually that is very common as shown in the following chat...

What is a guilty pleasure for you?

C: Chocolate.

P: What's your flavour? What's your go-to?

C: So back home (in Northern Ireland) Galaxies are my favourite.

P: Just the plain? Are we going big bar, or little bar?

C: Well, these days I'll go with the little bar, but back in the day, it used to be a big bar. I love Galaxy, I love chocolate. There's a company over here (U.S.A), or maybe it's there too Godiva. I love Godiva Chocolate.

P: Oh yes it is I know it. It's multi-coloured, isn't it? Is that the one?

C: No, it's gold, it's got a gold wrapper and so my guilty pleasure is chocolate. Sometimes I'll have a glass of red wine, a nice, fine red wine. What else is a guilty pleasure? That's it, and I don't even watch TV. Like I don't watch movies, I don't watch TV – unless it's something to do with the mind or it's a documentary. I'm obsessed with personal development. That's all I do and I study it every day.

People have said, *'Why should it be guilty? It's just pleasure.'* It is because the use of the word 'guilty' helps to create a context as it again speaks to non-judgement by creating a sense that even a guilty pleasure is okay to speak of, it creates space for people to say what they want to say. And a quick story on that. We used to ask people, 'Do you hear voices?' And people normally said, 'Hmm, that doesn't sound good if I'm hearing voices.' So we would ask; 'Okay, do you have an inner critic?' And most will answer, 'Oh yeah, I have an inner critic.'

In asking 'Do you hear voices?' we had unintentionally pre-determined a context for that question. When someone says, 'Yeah, I hear voices all time.' And people may go, 'Okay that's kind of crazy.' When we started to frame the question differently it allowed people to consider their own experience. For example if we ask; *'Do you tell yourself off? Do you have an inner critic?'* The answer is most often, 'Yeah, I do that all the time.' So very quickly we can ask in a way that most people will understand, they feel more comfortable and that is another way of creating a safe space for people.

In creating space to hear others, allowing time and in creating safety people may sometimes feel confused about times when they have felt talked at and that they haven't benefitted from an interaction. I would encourage people to consider the intention. During the Fire in the Belly interviews we are creating a space in terms of giving guests a safe space to talk, and we are also giving them explicit permission to do so. As host I am actively listening in terms of what they are saying and responding to their tone, the volume and pitch of their speech, noticing where they have looked, the way they have touched their throat because they are feeling restricted – visually listening.

We are looking to create space for positive and cathartic experiences. It is not a space to vent in terms of what has happened in the past - we are not allowing for negative talk, but we can have a cathartic experience by considering and sharing how and what we have learned from our life experiences.

In this space it is logical that people would love to talk because they have considered that they are going to have a safe space, time and they are asked to talk about their favourite subject - which is normally ourselves - their life story and what they have learned. And there is no expectation of them; they explicitly do not have to listen! They may only have been asked at most 10 questions over 90 minutes to two hours.

Here for you

We are giving that space as part of the process in order to build rapport, to feel connection and to show that as host I am hearing them. They are able to listen to themselves also, their own values and their needs. It is very appealing to us as human beings – that this other human being is hearing us and mirroring our values, wants and needs.

As an interviewer I actually find it easier; by creating space - a safe environment and protected time I am able to be fully focused and involved during the interview process. Ironically, outside of that environment, I'm not always a great listener. Ask my wife - but when I get the headphones on and sit before the microphone it is very much a case that this my only job, my only role for this dedicated time. And that is a key thing, you dedicate space and time, you're saying - I'm here for you.

'When you talk, you are only repeating what you know.
But if you really listen, you may learn something new.'

-Dalai Lama

Chapter Six

Non-Judgement

'An artist starts with a blank canvas, a musician starts with a blank page. The gift of listening is doing so with a blank mind.'

I have a question for you - When was the last time someone gave you the opportunity to talk without judgement in a safe space and in a positive way?

The immediate reaction when we first ask this question is often that the answer is never and we don't think that's uncommon, most people may understand that they have been given safe spaces in a number of different areas but not in a wholly non-judgemental way and there are reasons for that.

We may have a conversation with a friend over a period of time, is it a safe space? Normally Yes. Is it a non-judgmental space? Maybe and Maybe not. That's not a reflection on our friends or whoever we're speaking to, it's simply that mostly we talk to our partners, our family, our close friends and often those around us have preconceived ideas of who we are, who we were as a child or what we did previously. They have knowledge of our past and it may be very hard for them to be neutral. It may be that we've done something before, so they will be slightly pre-meditated. For example, if you are naturally a gifted writer, they may say well; 'it's fine for you because you can just write.'

That's a judgement, it's a positive judgement, in terms of them being aware of your past history but that doesn't necessarily tell you how you actually feel about it. You can be good at something but it doesn't mean that your passion is attached to it - it doesn't mean your energy flows there.

Ikigai

In non-judgement we can consider how we actually feel about something and where our energy flows to. In chapter four we talked briefly about the Japanese process of Ikigai, which although it doesn't have a direct translation in English, is a concept that means 'a reason for being.' Ikigai refers to having a meaningful direction or purpose in life. It is the sense of our life being made worthwhile, with actions taken toward achieving our Ikigai resulting in satisfaction and a sense of meaning to life. It's the reason that we jump out of bed.

It could be that actually you're happy doing the things that you're good at. It could be a blockage for you that may have kept you doing the things that you are good at rather than following your goals but when you're there to hear someone talk in a safe space you must set the intention to provide a very positive non-judgmental environment. That means that you just let them talk, know that it's not a feedback environment – on the Show oftentimes we almost don't need to respond.

Ikigai sets some vital questions that require us to set our judgement aside;

What do you love?

What are you good at?

What does the world need?

What can you get paid well for?

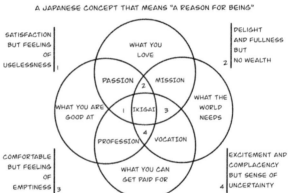

IKIGAI
A JAPANESE CONCEPT THAT MEANS "A REASON FOR BEING"

SATISFACTION
BUT FEELING
OF
USELESSNESS 1

DELIGHT
AND FULLNESS
BUT
NO WEALTH 2

WHAT YOU LOVE

PASSION

MISSION

2

WHAT YOU ARE GOOD AT

1 IKIGAI 3

WHAT THE WORLD NEEDS

4

PROFESSION

VOCATION

COMFORTABLE
BUT FEELING
OF
EMPTINESS 3

WHAT YOU CAN GET PAID FOR

EXCITEMENT AND
COMPLACENCY
BUT SENSE OF
UNCERTAINTY 4

As host I have found that a non-judgemental space is one of the key powers of the Show. Over time I have learned that I can provide a non-judgemental environment for myself when I go within and for others. So by suspending the conversation in this positive space, by sitting at a microphone and having a set of headphones on the guest will often feel that they've got to be cautious in terms of how this is reflected and picked up by somebody in the outside world.

It's a bit flattering for the ego too as we're here to learn about their insights, so straight away we've actually guided the discussion and that it needs to be both positive and constructive so that other people outside can maybe understand it or benefit from it. It is an opportunity to explain yourself and you are being listened to and heard without judgement.

The next step in terms of the guest agreeing to release their life story is critical as, once you have put it out there - once it is released so that other people can hear it then others may potentially judge you. The guest must be willing and able for that to happen.

Getting past the conscious

The first 20 – 30 minutes is typically when people are talking consciously - it's almost like a premeditated script in their head – I hear what they normally say, their style and really this is what they know *how they will be judged on*. But then after that time people normally relax, just sit back a bit and start to enjoy the chance to stretch their mental wings a bit and it suspends the conversation in a beautiful state and we're here until the interview comes to a natural end. The guest is being heard both without and within, each question allows them to search within and, once we get past the conscious responses, the guest has now experienced that the host is not there to judge them. They are not having to process how the other person may be judging them or even consider what the other person may be thinking. For some the interview will last 60 minutes and for some it's three hours. I trust that whatever happens is right for the guest, the human being in front of me.

As the interviewer I can spot the changes in their tone as they move past their conscious responses the person actually sits back in the chair and often their tone drops. If they're a fast speaker then it tends to slow down and suddenly they become very methodical because the conversation is coming straight from the subconscious. I will see them note something that they have just said and they may think - that's interesting, what I've just said, where I can actually sit back with a bag of popcorn and just listen to what they are saying.

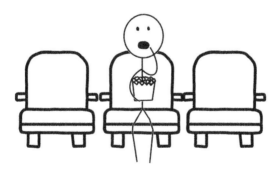

To be able to be heard in a non-judgemental space can create a kind of semi-out of body experience for the guests - it's like going to the cinema and watching yourself. For many guests they naturally start to go within and question themselves within the interview – they will start to explore, *'...all right I said that why would I say that?'* and that's what gives us as people the ability also to separate ourselves from our conscious thoughts and also our egos.

The Chimp

A favourite book of mine is 'The Chimp Paradox' by Professor Steve Peters. It talks about the Chimp Mind, or the ego as many of us would call it, and shares useful tools to manage your mind. One of my mentoring clients sent me a painting of a chimp wearing red lipstick and a bikini. And for me that is how my internal Chimp now looks, if I am going to have this Chimp, this ego and critic, running around inside my head - well at least I can dress it up!

You can do this, you can think of your Chimp, in those times when you may feel overwhelmed by emotions or fearful of being judged as simply your Chimp mind rattling a cage in lipstick and a bikini. Instead of judging ourselves or another person, instead of saying I'm angry I can say my Chimp is angry, so straight away I've disassociated. I can step back from my Chimp and ask why have I reacted to a situation or experience in this way? I fully accept that I have a Chimp and we all need our Chimp because it will often help to keep us safe. We can manage our Chimp however and for me seeing the futility of a chimp in lipstick and a bikini works almost every time.

I have decided that if I'm going have a chimp running around in my head and we are together for life I may as well make it look pretty, or smart or funny.

So here comes my chimp with really badly applied makeup in a bikini.

It is in being in a state of non-judgement that the Chimp can be more relaxed nine times out of ten. In providing a non-judgemental space the Chimp can understand that the other person is not trying to trample across our value set, in fact if anyone's doing that then it is most probably us in that type of environment.

POINTING THE FINGER

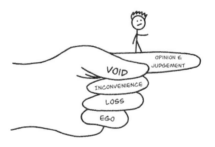

In this way we can reconsider the past and our experiences. We have the power to change the past. Read that again. *Does it challenge you?* Good. The past lives in our imagination and I have found this from my own experience:

'Around the age of 12 years, I was basically having a bit of a hard time in school. In some ways it wasn't that serious, but I got myself in a bit of trouble at school and for me it really felt like I was isolated and it led to thoughts and feelings of suicide. And things that were going on in my perception at the time was that my parents weren't supporting me, the school was against me, it's me against the world. It was at an age and a time in young people's lives anyway where it's incredibly vulnerable. Not that long ago as young kids we have believed in the Tooth Fairy and Santa Claus then suddenly friends and parents are telling us to grow up and you're having to go through all this transition. At the time I harboured those feelings and I had those for a long, long time, my entire life up until I reached 37 and a half years of age, so some 25 years.

However, when I went back to look at it through being mentored, therapy, learning to face my internal challenges and being provided with the space to look at it without judgement - to look at it and ask myself, *'do you really think your parents didn't know?'* And it's like, actually do you know what, I was choosing, not choosing to be isolated but it was my perception that I was isolated at that time. In talking to my sister, she was there and she witnessed that my parents were worried about me. But my perception at the time was that I was on my own and they were against me. And it wasn't true, not at all. It was a communication thing. The school were doing what they felt was best as, like a lot of things, things changed through time. For me moving into a space of non-judgement has allowed me to frame my experiences in a way that I can learn and grow from them.'

The state of being and listening in non-judgement is the gift of providing a blank canvas to the other. Judgement is always about our own needs, values and reactions. It is the gift of listening that provides the other with the gift of being heard, it is an essential part of the process that allows people to frame their life stories, experiences and the events that have shaped them in a way that allows for understanding, learning and growth.

'When you judge another you do not define them, you

define yourself.'

-   **Dr Wayne Dyer**

There is an old story that I would like to share, Who Knows?, which perfectly illustrates how being in a state of non-judgement of the events that happen in our lives can allow us to accept the present experience and allow it to unfold as it will without the need for control over the outcome. It shows us how to not judge our experiences or the views of another as good or bad.

Who Knows?

This is an old Chinese story about a rice farmer who lived a very simple life. He had a small home and a few children. He had a small field of rice that was just enough to feed and provide for his family. And one day a herd of wild horses came running through the village and ran into his rice field and got stuck in the mud and they couldn't get away so they were his.

His neighbour came running over and said, 'This is good news! Such good fortune! You are rich, this is amazing!' And the rice farmer said, 'Good news, bad news, who knows?'

And a few weeks later his son that was twelve years old decided to jump on one of the wild horses for a ride and very shortly the wild horse throws him off and he breaks his leg. The neighbour comes running over and says, 'Oh no, this is such bad news!' And the farmer said, 'Good news, bad news, who knows?'

A week later a Chinese general is marching through his village with the army to go to war. And on this march to war going through villages, they would take every boy that was over ten years old that was healthy. So they took every boy in the village that was healthy except his son because he had a broken leg.

The neighbour comes running over and says, 'Yes! This is wonderful news, how lucky are we!' And the father replies, 'Good news, bad news, who knows?'

And that is the end of the story but that is how the life is—*who knows?*

Chapter Seven

No Agenda

'Hear the other person's values, beliefs and experiences;
in listening allow no agenda.'

One of the first questions we asked when starting the Fire In The Belly Show, and that you may have asked on reading the chapter title, was; *'Can you have no agenda?'*

We start our interviews on the show with a blank A3 page, a clear and blank space and withhold inputs. As an engineer, and through that training for much of my life, as show host I felt the need to have lists and to have or create structure in some ways I was always setting an agenda, a plan. And there are many places for that but I have learned that there is no place for an agenda when we set the intention to hear or be heard.

BLANK CANVAS – EVERYTHING & NOTHING

If have we no agenda then we have the opportunity as the listener to hold and be the mirror, to reflect what we experience through them and act as a mirror for where the guest is most comfortable, uncomfortable or has a moment of clarity. The guest or other may feel that the listener resonates with what they are saying; but as the listener, whilst this may or may not be true, we can still hold the space and just listen.

Noise

There are so many ways to get our messages heard these days but what or whose agenda are we hearing? Are you aware any longer what is a sponsored message, an affiliate post, a lead magnet or pre-meditated communication which follows an industry system to trigger our mental faculties through the choice of wording, tone and frequency. And that is not a judgement of their agenda just an observation that many times an agenda is present to get us to buy something or act in a certain way. The old marketing rule of 7 i.e. that it takes an average of 7 points of contact before you buy a brand or item has been replaced by the rule of 27 – that it takes generating your message at least 27 times before a buyer or potential client will feel they resonate with, or even remember, your brand. When a message is being marketed through advertising or social media it is purposely pushed out to you. It could be question-based marketing, it could be emotive and trying to get you to feel, it could be fear-based marketing; whatever it is the agenda is to paint a picture and ultimately get you to buy or at least listen and connect to a certain message.

Social media algorithms are working to show you the best options based on your previous activity and potentially provide you with a two way communication so that you can be an observer or have the option to interact. With social media and with many social interactions, there are different layers of listening where you may hear an open, helpful message or you may find yourself waiting for an action, for the link at the bottom of the post. Quite often people hear a fear-based message because currently fear often sells a hell of a lot better than positive messaging. We are not knocking selling, in our opinion we are all salespeople when it comes to getting our needs and values met. As people we are normally interacting and sharing our messages with an overt or covert agenda. Ideally we try to get what we want and if it's a win-win situation, then in return, we will give you what you want.

'The gift of listening is doing so with a blank mind.'

It is in tearing up any such agenda that we can create the opportunity to really hear the other person. On the Fire in the Belly show we are interviewing the guests but, without any agenda, it is a very different type of interview. The guest is not being assessed, nor are we seeking more detail on any particular topic, we don't want to catch them out and we are not aiming for any type of exclusive.

We purposefully do not want the guest to become triggered and by that we mean stuck in a negative loop of shame and the FOG of fear, obligation and guilt. In order to minimise the risk of this we will have purposely asked them to consider things that they don't want to discuss and ask only that they don't discuss them. If they do they can choose not to release the interview and they can also do the interview again at a later date.

NEGATIVE INFINITY LOOP

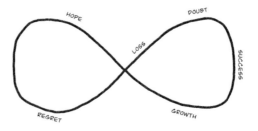

The Fire in the Belly show has chosen to hear what they have to say about their values, beliefs and experiences. We do not edit the interviews after the show is recorded. Apart from being checked for gaps or noise, they're not shortened nor are bits taken. On the show there is no agenda because we only want to hear from that person and their own life story. That is the only assurance that we provide - that the interview will not be edited, so that it cannot be taken even slightly out of context because our aim is that it fully represents the guest. Our only fear was that someone would at any point feel or say, 'I don't recognise my own story,' due to any editing process.

That integrity is of vital importance to us on the show, it is one of our top core values and we want our guests to go away and be confident to say, 'This is me. This is my story. I laid my heart on the line, and that's okay.'

In having no underlying plan or aim for the guests on the show we afford them the opportunity to speak from experience and share openly. In having no agenda or a blank agenda, if you will, we go where we go. And that's okay.

Mirror

As host I am using many of the traits of counselling in the form of listening, mirroring and allowing verbal flow which can often enable the guest to get insight or understanding by reflecting on their lessons but it is most definitely not counselling and it is on public record. Talking about the actions of any other persons is not encouraged and in particular any naming and shaming is not allowed, and we are not there with the intention to achieve change.

The focus is on listening and we may observe patterns and seek understanding through asking clarifying questions. We want to see and hear the guest as clearly as we can, to hold up a mirror and listen to our own feelings in translating the guest's message. It may be appropriate to say that you are feeling something, for example, *do you ever find yourself listening to someone and it doesn't feel right or you can't understand that how you are feeling may not match with what they are saying or the way that they are saying it?*

As a listener and certainly as host on the show, if a guest is talking about an experience we may feel excitement or nausea or sadness. In the role of host on the show I will always clarify this with the guest and may ask the guest to explain things again in a different way; the aim is clarity and to offer an echo chamber so that they can hear their own words.

This often provides a disruption to the guests, a moment of questioning and compassion to cause a break so that they can step back and explore their own message and experience.

'In standing back we allow a blank canvas, hold a mirror and allow the other to reflect on their journey.'

In having no set agenda we can observe things – we look for the words being said, the tone being used and their body-language as we let the story unfold and allow them to self-reflect as it runs its course. In choosing to just listen to another we just may get the fortunate opportunity to walk a mile in someone else's shoes.

'If you were to fully and truly listen, and only form an opinion when you have heard all the facts, then you would likely never have an opinion.'

The Big Pause

The power of the pause is a useful tool to encourage and allow people to speak freely – we call it the Big Pause or the Big Paws. On the show much of the host responses are in using the pause to allow the guest to finish, expand or identify what they are saying or want to say next.

'All excellent listeners are masters of the pause. They are comfortable with silences.'

- **Brian Tracy**

This is not to be confused with any idea of a dramatic pause to hammer home a point but rather to allow people to finish talking, to say all they have to say, to let them talk it out and not interrupt.

We have no agenda over what they may be saying or not saying but in providing the big pause we can be sure that we have not inadvertently changed the direction of their thinking or the story that they are sharing.

After the show it is a common experience for guests to come back on or get in touch to tell us that they have had a shift in their lives or have reached a new awareness on a relationship, experience or connection in their lives. The truth is that when we listen back to the shows the audience can often recognise some small part of ourselves in each guest. In many industries there will always be a third party, an interface between a client and the supplier. In the construction world that may be a client agent who is there to visually observe and be the objective listener. Consider;

Can you set aside any agenda that you have over your own life story?

What might you learn about yourself and your current situation?

A good place to start may be in answering, without agenda, some of the top Fire in the Belly Questions.

These questions have repeatedly caused some of the most reflective answers and learning for guests. Take the time to answer each one in terms of what it means for you today. These questions can also be useful to revisit regularly.

9 Fire In The Belly Questions to ask yourself, without agenda!

1.   What does Fire in the Belly mean to you?

2.   What are your core values?

3.   What is your superpower?

9 Fire In The Belly Questions to ask yourself, without agenda!

4.   If you were to write a book, what would it be about?

5.   What surprise talent, ability, skill or feature do you have?

6.   What do you love to do?

9 Fire In The Belly Questions to ask yourself, without agenda!

7.   What gets you going in the morning?

8.   What is your definition of success?

9.   Who or what is your biggest inspiration?

9 Fire In The Belly Questions to ask yourself, without agenda!

Bonus Question: In ten years' time, when you look back, what will you say about what you are doing now?

Chapter Eight

Power of Listening

'When people talk, listen completely. Most people never listen.'

- **Ernest Hemmingway**

Listening is a skill that people can learn; both to listen to somebody else and it is most powerful when we learn to listen to ourselves. Going within to hear ourselves is to listen to what we have to say, to hear what we actually think. It is the ability to listen to ourselves consciously in terms of our previous experiences and then also subconsciously in terms of learning to identify or trust our gut instinct, our intuition. Listening in itself is often not necessarily auditory, as in through your ears.

In listening, sometimes it's about the words, more often it's the actual word we use together with the tone, the context, the reflection and the attitude behind it.

If someone says; 'I have to go to work,' when we break that down, 'have' is a very laboured word and it's an order. If they say 'I want to go to work.' Then it's slightly different there's a choice and you're choosing to do it and you're stepping ahead of it. So, it's not about the necessity, it's more than that.

If you then take the same thing and you change it to, 'I love to go to work' then love is an extremely passionate word. The word love goes straight to your heart and it's a very positive thing to say. The outcome is the same as the person goes to work but for them and for the person listening, they are having a different experience. Each word brings a very different feeling both for the person talking and the person listening.

In order to have a quiet and deep conversation people will first find a quiet place and it is there in the language, 'let's go sit down somewhere quiet and talk.' The power of listening comes in letting someone talk without judgement. In choosing to listen you are a facilitator for another person's story and in every question to simply ask in order to understand the other correctly, as they intend.

Actively listening is saying, *'can you tell me what that means to you?'*

It is useful to use open questions and reflect back what you have heard in order to seek clarity and ensure that you have a translation and not an interpretation. On the show as host we will ask the question for example something; *'When you said that I am getting mixed feelings, does that mean anything to you?'*

It is in the translation that we evolve the mirror into a diamond and hear through the spectrum of actively listening to the others experience, tone and communication style. In translating we are able to get as close as possible to the experience or message of the person we are listening to.

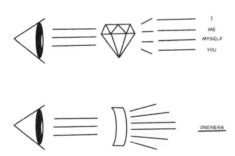

It is useful to understand the type of communication style when listening to others. If you listen to a movie in a foreign language you can still often understand the meaning from the tone, how the person is speaking and the facial expressions. There can be understanding without hearing the actual words and how much we hear the actual words said is related to our own communication style. There is a simple way to identify how someone best learns and communicates and that is through the VAK model, often referred to within NLP or neuro-linguistic programming.

Visual, Auditory, and Kinaesthetic Communication and Learning Styles

Used with permission from the NLP Coaching Practitioner Training, © Tad and Adriana James and The Tad James Co.

Confusion and misunderstandings happen for many reasons. The message sent is not necessarily the one received. People communicate, both verbally and nonverbally, in a diversity of styles. It's almost as if they're speaking different languages to each   other.

There are many communication models. This particular one, from the field of Neuro-linguistic Programming (NLP), is commonly known as **VAK (Visual, Auditory, and Kinaesthetic)**. NLP can tell us and teach us a lot about how we use the language of the mind to consistently achieve our specific and desired outcomes.

The nervous system (the mind) through which our experience is processed is via 5 senses with the first three **VAK** being the predominant:

Visual – people with visual bias normally sit or stand with head and eyes up and bodies straight. Appearance is very important to them and they most often think in pictures and appearances. Language used for example – in view of, looks like, well defined

Auditory - people with this bias learn by listening and can normally repeat things back to you easily. People with this bias normally will talk to themselves and like to listen to music and talk on the phone or video calls. Language used for example – voiced an opinion, word for word, described in details

Kinaesthetic – people with this learning and communication style will normally talk and move quite slowly, they memorise by doing or 'walking through' a subject. Language used for example – start from scratch, hang in there, get to grips with

Also for consideration:

Olfactory – smells can bring back memories or support memory function. Language used for example – I can smell victory, I can smell fear, fresh

Gustatory – when people talk about how something tasted. Language used for example – that is sweet, get a taste of things to come

The VAK model was developed by psychologists in the 1920's and is used by educators, trainers and psychologists globally today. It is particularly useful for people who struggled through a traditional school system in order to learn more about how they actually learn. Here is a simple illustration:

`A guest on the show may say I would love to drive a red Porsche. In order to understand fully I might ask *what size, what shape? And when you say drive, are you talking high speed or cruising? Are you talking roof down?* And by the time you drill down, drill down and drill down, they're literally painting their picture and we are understanding their picture, so that we can understand their reflection of the world.

In listening to someone the power is in making sure that you have the most detailed picture of their experience or message, almost taken from their mind through their description and that you've been able to paint that in your own world.

So now in painting a picture you can better understand the other person. And if they say, 'I love to drive fast.' Okay, *why do you love to go fast?* 'It's just the freedom, the thrill, the excitement, the energy.' I am starting to get all the core words and identify the key things for them. I can see that their smile is ear to ear. In talking about their passion or something that they love the guest is normally really buzzing with high energy, they're very animated and very vocal.

CONSCIOUS SENSES

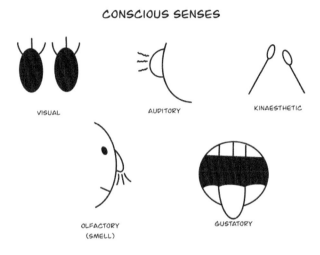

In such a conversation I will have learned if the person I am listening to is visual, auditory or kinaesthetic.

In the above example on driving, if they are auditory I will hear, 'I love to hear the sound of the engine and all the noises and the wind whooshing past me.'

Or they might say, 'I love looking at the car, its colour and shape and seeing all the countryside go past me,' straightaway we know they have a visual bias.

If they are kinaesthetic they might say, 'Oh, it feels so good. I love to touch the steering wheel and the feeling of the wind in my hair.'

It can also be a mixture of these three main communication styles, but generally people are all biased in some shape or form.'

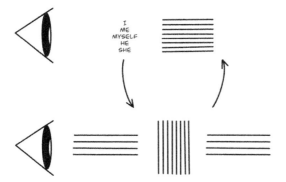

One guest G shared how he uses his visual bias mixed with kinaesthetic:

P: (from the conversation to that point...) You are obviously quite picture focused - very visually biased.

G: Yes, (I have) practised visualisation for a long time now. I want to see it... I want to know how it feels when I'm there, which is very deep visualisation. A lot of people go, 'Oh, I can visualise that car!' and they look at a picture of a car, however okay, you can visualise because you just looked at it. You know what a BMW X-5 looks like, or you know what that holiday looks - you've been on a holiday. But I don't, I like to go. I like to go there and feel it.

I have visualised myself welcoming people to an event, and know how immensely proud I feel. I visualise myself standing there looking out to people and the rush that it gives me. I can visualise standing in America doing an event. Think Inspiration USA or whatever it might be. I can visualise that. I can visualise standing there, welcoming people and visualising that feeling that it gives me; I can actually go there in my mind and feel that feeling. And I think that's the most powerful form of visualising.

P: How do you do that for other people?

G: Inspire them and help paint the picture for them? Exactly what I'm doing right now, I think through my Network. I think that we are the change that needs to happen. And we'll continue to do it. And the more I learn, the more it will improve as well.

'It just is, until we decide what it is.'

When we know and can use another's learning and communication style they will feel listened to because we are using their language. For example, we can think in terms of further questions, prompting someone and how we frame our questions that best show we are listening to them and that will help them best listen to themselves; *'How does that sound to you? Or how does that look to you? Or again, how would it feel to do that?'*

On the Fire in the Belly show we allow two hours per interview and they average 90 minutes plus, so they generally aren't short. And that's for a number of reasons as outlined in this book. What is almost universal is that in the post-interview chat when we are off-air and off camera guests will say, 'that was an amazing conversation.' And yet it wasn't a conversation, it was an unusual interview, in that the guests were there to be listened to.

The goal of listening to them on the show is to learn about their life story and their reflections on their lessons and successes. The power of listening is to watch the movie of their life as they talk you through it.

Guests have the opportunity to really talk and go in depth and think about what they're saying, what they want to say and the power of listening is to sit back- we can have a slightly out of body view on it and say let's look at this situation – *what are they actually saying?*

When you see a very young child and they are upset, as an adult we may be able to step back and understand that something has brought up a strong reaction for them. That young child will shout and scream to be listened to if they have to. A very young child doesn't have the same power of words yet and their communication may have been misheard so it can escalate very quickly. As the adult or parent in the room we will try to focus, to really listen to what the child is saying or communicating to through their tone and body language - internally we often start to go through a list of questions; *'are they tired? Is it this food? Was there something they really wanted to do? Maybe it's because they haven't got the language – can they point to what they want?'*

We are using all of those things that we've learned in terms of active listening and visual cues and although the child mightn't be able to tell us what they want or need, we're trying to work through it with them to discover what it could be. When we are actively listening to them we can help them in ways that resolve any issues and reassure the child. Having young children has reinforced my experience of potential positives in the power of listening; in my own home it's my wife's skill, to be honest and her ability to sort of almost talk me down. It's weird because it's so close I almost can't see it. When people say, 'How is it you can listen to somebody for two hours and really understand them, yet your kids when they're yelling at you, you can't see it.'

And that's the power of having a mediator in between you and the topic, person or an issue. On the show it's the microphone, fact that we are recording and the protected space. It's not uncommon that people say, the best place to have an in-depth conversation is in the car on a long journey. There are a number of things that enable you to listen including the structure of facing forward. The space of the car acts like an enclosure and you are both looking forward in the same direction. People will say 'God, we've not talked like this in ages,' or will say, 'they actually listened.'

'Most people do not listen with the intent to understand;

they listen with the intent to reply.'

- **Stephen R Covey**

One guest was motivated, following the powerful experience of being listened to on the Fire in the Belly show, to listen to a loved one and shared their outcome by email afterwards. During their life story talk they had found insight into how they might improve a key relationship in their life and more importantly a burning desire to reconnect and reshape this connection. The experience of being listened to on the show had inspired and empowered them with a potential new tool and they took action, writing afterwards to the show as outlined on the next page.

This guest had talked about a family tragedy and its impact on the family; recently there had been an incident whereby a sibling had cut themselves off from the rest of the family completely. Writing to the host a few weeks later the guest said:

'Lockdown and varying rules in 2020 had made face to face visits really challenging so I said to heck, I'm going down for a visit, no matter what.

I had talked your (Fire In The Belly) podcast through with one of my other siblings for two hours the previous Sunday. I got my head around how to approach my difficult conversation.

I got in the car and for three hours I listened, really listened.

I didn't do my older sibling ...thing, I didn't put my solution hat on, and I really tuned in and listened. I had one of the most profound experiences of my life. And this sibling is back texting me and connecting again.

That makes me really happy, not in a smiley way, in a personally fulfilled way – it's a great big rip that's been darned and made strong again.

I wanted you to know the effect that meeting you has had on my life.'

-   C.

In being listened to this guest learned first-hand of the power of being listened to and used their experience, both the learning and the insights gained. On the show they discussed how much they missed this connection and its importance to them and to their lives. They had had, like many of us may experience, a total relationship breakdown with this person and on the show they found the understanding that they wanted to find a way to mend the rip that had torn them apart. In taking action and choosing to listen, to listen fully, to just listen they had what they call the most profound experience of their lives.

Human connection is critical to us all as human beings. The following story is one guests experience of listening and of being listened to. It speaks of the life-changing difference that it can make and its place in each of our relationships, both with self and others.

The power of listening was a revelation to this guest who was surprised at their own surprise saying:

'You would think, I would know my story pretty smoothly, but no, there's still lots of, 'Oh my gosh. And then I did this and then I did that moments.'

I appreciate you letting me come on the (Fire In The Belly) show because this is, this is refreshing and eye opening - as a counsellor and a life coach, usually I'm the one listening and asking the questions so it's fun to spin it on its head.'

Discovering that she was a lesbian in her mid-20's was a process in listening to herself:

'....Communication wasn't my forte when I was younger and I would say, with my daughter, it's almost like I'm teaching her how to do it right. But when you interact with people from your past and from when you were younger, you kind of revert back. So I just wrote my Mum a snail mail about what was going on and you know, I'm gay and I wrote that it doesn't mean I'm going to have rainbow hair and be a completely different person. I'm still the exact same person.

I probably kept it short and sweet. I'm not; I'm not a huge writer. I sent that and I think there might've been a week in between before hearing anything back.

Who knows what she said to other people and who knows the conversations she had with my brother or her sister but she, it's not like she tried to talk me out of it or if she did I have blocked that out because I'm deliriously happy now so I don't, I don't remember that...

I was 27 by then and had just come out of a marriage and I was still a people pleaser…. I still had to learn…. So now I was in my first relationship with a woman and it was toxic.

You always hear about counsellors and healers and people like that, needing their own therapy and not listening to themselves and I'm totally for that support. That's why counsellors have counsellors and coaches have coaches and highly successful people ask for help and get the help they need. So gosh, it was probably three years or so with this relationship that was just nothing that I would want for my kid. Nothing. And it's not on either one of us because I'm sure she went on to find her person and is happy now, I hope, but you know sometimes there's just incompatibility.

After that, there was about a year of, You know what, I'm going to stop looking so hard and I'm just going to hang out with my friends, which again, I'd never been single long enough to do.

So I just enjoyed watching movies and going to concerts and just laughing and having fun and kind of figuring out a little more of who I was. And then finally a close friend set me up with my special someone.

A.

This guest uses the power of listening every day in their counselling and coaching work and knows well the benefits of listening to others. It is in the power of listening to herself that she has demonstrated her ability to change her life and influence others and, like many of us, continue to find surprise in what she calls the 'eye-opening and refreshing' experience of being listened to.

'I've learned that people will forget what you said, people will forget what you did, but people will never forget how you made them feel.'

-Maya Angelou

In times when we are nursing someone or they have a particular illness or condition like cancer or dementia, as their condition progresses due to medications or the effects on their brain they may forget who we are. A person we love not recognising us is a very difficult thing for many of us to go through. The messaging from dementia charities is often that if it comes to that point to focus on how we're making the person feel because even though they might not recognise us, we can still engender good feelings within them.

A story on feeling

A woman had a close relationship with her aunt who had developed advanced dementia. Her aunt had stopped recognising her as her niece. The aunt's husband was dead. The niece now did all of the household things; she always organised for the grass to be cut, for the window cleaner to come.

Over time her aunt started calling her by her husband's name.   The niece was very upset and it was very confusing for her. However when she looked at it, really listened to what her aunt was communicating to her and thought about how she was making her aunt feel - it made perfect sense. The reason? The reason was that although the aunt often didn't recognise her and no longer remembered her name, the feelings the niece brought up within her aunt were feelings of being looked after, being protected, being cared for. She was doing the things for her that the aunt's husband had done, many of the things that traditionally a man would quite often do. And in understanding this and in listening to what her aunt was actually communicating, their relationship took on a different and a new quality.

In invoking these feelings in someone that they feel secure, they recognise you, it's a warm connection and they're not afraid. We aren't on the conscious physical world anymore, the person doesn't recognise our face or name perhaps but they're listening in terms of the energy that we are giving off. In considering how we are making the other feel - if by listening to what they are communicating and through our presence we are creating in them a sense of warmth and caring, that can be enough.

Chapter Nine

Hearing voices

'For me my inner voice is the quietest little whisper, that does not repeat itself, and is often only heard on long walks and in the shower.'

Guests often say that they have heard themselves whilst on the Fire in the Belly show and as illustrated in the previous chapter sometimes they will find clarity on some topic, issue or memory in their lives whilst sharing their life story.   In offering time and space we make a connection with the guest using empathetic listening, meaning that we pay attention to them and what they are saying, we seek to understand.

After the first 30 minutes most guests will start to enter a state of flow and it is in this space that we find guests will start to go off-script and speak from their subconscious mind. On the Fire in the Belly show it is the role of the interviewer to facilitate their story. It is to occupy the interface between the person and their soul.

In order to hear ourselves we have to go within to find and actively listen to our inner voice or voices; our intuition if you will. On the show we see it clearly and regularly demonstrated that for most people this inner voice is in actual fact an inner critic. What has been a surprise for the team and for our guests is the level of comfort and acceptance that most people have for their inner critic.

Do you hear voices?

When we started the show we asked people did they talk to themselves and that made people really uncomfortable. They would consider it as, and even say that's; 'kind of like something a psychologist or therapist would say to me, and I would be afraid that I'm about to get locked up.'

Whereas if you say to someone, *do you have an inner critic?* The response is emphatic and instant from 95% of guests – 'Oh, yes, I have got one of those.'

When you read this - whose voice do you hear?

What do you think of this voice? Is it one voice or multiple?

I asked this at the start of the book and I ask you to reflect on it once again. We find then that people are hearing themselves but rather than hearing a supportive inner voice many of us are living with multiple inner critics who are judging, pointing the finger and criticising our choices.

It can be a running inner dialogue where you are chatting away to yourself. That can be one and the same voice if you can strip away all the distraction and the noise. For example, if we are watching social media our inner voice could be talking in a way that is criticising either ourselves – 'I wouldn't look good in that,' or it could be criticising the other – 'I wouldn't wear that.'

Hearing the answers

For one guest by asking questions and going within as a young child she revealed that she heard the answers but not as a voice:

'So I'm originally from Derry in Northern Ireland. And I grew up in a pretty; I would say it was a dysfunctional upbringing. My mother left when I was, I think I was two years old and she left to go to America to try and make a better life for our family. She was a single mom at the time. And my grandparents raised me and my siblings. My grandmother was the head of the household. She was the queen of the family.

My father really wasn't involved. He would come and go and we'd see him sometimes, sometimes we wouldn't. He always showed up at Christmas in some way shape or form, but then he'd disappear again. And we wouldn't see him for maybe months, sometimes years. So I didn't grow up with a normal childhood and it wasn't easy.

Looking back, it was not an easy childhood, it was hard. I longed for my mother very much. I would cry for her, I missed her.

I didn't understand why was I different from my friends? Why did they have their mommy and daddy?

Going to school, and that hurt because, you would see your friend's parents come into the school, when they have school meetings.

I remember always feeling alone in those moments and thinking, why am I different?

And it's interesting, I go back on that journey and I've healed a lot from the pain of not having parents growing up but when I look back at it, I think that that's where my deep faith and spirituality came from.

When I was young, when I was probably like six or seven years of age, I remember crying for my mother and my father and asking questions.

I would just talk to God and in my mind and my heart, and I would say, God, why am I alone? Why don't I have a mother? Why don't I have a father? And, I always got this answer, Well, I'm your father. And it wasn't a voice, I wasn't hearing voices, but it was just a thought, right. I'm your father.

As far back as I remember, I think I was seven, I've always said, God is my father. God is my father, and that doesn't mean Jesus. That doesn't mean a religious figure. It's just God, it's Universe, and it's Almighty.'

-   C.O.

On the Fire and the Belly Show by the time people start to talk from their subconscious mind and use their inner voice they have already been telling their story for upwards of 30 minutes and the environment of the show has allowed the removal of stimulation in terms of other people, social media, other's ideas or opinions. If we consider why people say, 'I come up with my best ideas in the shower. I come up with my best ideas when I go for a walk or as I am falling asleep?'

The reason is often that in the shower, on a walk or in bed ready to sleep we have removed all of the external stimulation and at that time we are able to hear our inner voice or may hear a message within.

In these times we are both talking to and listening to ourselves. Depending on our mental wellness, current life events and levels of understanding the inner voice may be a constant stream of chatter or it may be clearer and more defined.

If we are on a walk, for example, and our mind - rather than switching off or being able to focus on the trees and nature - may suddenly respond and start to search for stimulation. It may look back to an experience and start to unpick it and wonder; why did another say something to you last week and start to question the reasons for that. When people have time to think through what happened, what was said, what was done and then we can start to get into the deeper questions. On the show guests are bringing the insights and lessons that they have learned from their own life story up to that point in time. In looking back at their experiences and listening to the understanding that they have gained, quite often in the moment by listening to themselves.

WHERE DOES YOUR INNER VOICE NARRATE FROM?

One guest revealed how a near death experience had led him to experience a spiritual awakening and start to completely change his life;

'I had a medical emergency…(I was in agonising pain and believed that I may be dying.) At the hospital they put me on one of those trolleys and they're wheeling me down to X-ray because they thought it was a blockage in the stomach… all the way down to X-ray it was like the whole world just stopped.

I was encapsulated in this amazing feeling of love, energy and connection - nothing like I'd ever had before. At that point I just thought, wow, what's going on? There was no man with a beard but there was a living, conscious, loving energy that was surrounding me and within me… nothing like I'd ever felt before and there's no voice, but there's kind of like an inner knowing of a message being sent to me saying, 'you're going to be fine, but you need to change your life in some way or form.'

The next minute I'm waking up in X-ray and I'm suddenly really feeling a lot better. And within, I think, four or five hours, I was out of the hospital and I had had this kind of like spiritual experience, obviously… I felt I had to give back in some way or form.'

- D.G

ROCK THROWER   **VS**   PEACE KEEPER

Why?

We will often ask the guests about their why? In finding our fire in the belly, our passion and our why it is essential that we listen to ourselves and those why questions are a way for us to go within and hear our inner voice(s). There is a simple exercise that the team on the show have used and that we sometimes use with guests or may refer them to after the show.

It is called The 7 Levels Deep Exercise and it is provided here for you to complete to help you find your *why?*

Identifying our why is essential to know that, whatever we are choosing to do, we are doing for the right reasons so that we don't get to the point of suddenly filling that value and discovering that actually it wasn't what we really wanted. It was just a void in our life. So why not ask the question, *what is my Why?*

The 7 Levels Deep Exercise Can Be Used For Any Topic, Issue, Need or Want!

This exercise is to help you find your **Why?**

1. What is important to you about achieving the ideal you? What is important to you about becoming / being / doing

   _____? (write in what it is you want)

   ┌───┐
   │ (Write why it is important in this box)   │
   │   │
   │   │
   │   │
   │   │
   └───┘

2. Enter your answer from the above box in this question –

   Why is it important for you to _____?

   ┌───┐
   │ (Write why it is important in this box)   │
   │   │
   │   │
   │   │
   │   │
   └───┘

3.   Enter your answer from the above box in this question –

Why is it important for you to _____?

(Write why it is important in this box)

4.   Enter your answer from the above box in this question –

Why is it important for you to _____?

(Write why it is important in this box)

5.   Enter your answer from the above box in this question –

Why is it important for you to _____?

(Write why it is important in this box)

6. Enter your answer from the above box in this question - Specifically, why is it important for you to

_____?

(Write why it is important in this box)

7. Enter your answer from the above box in this question

Why is it important for you to _____?

My Big **Why** Is:

WHAT IS IMPORTANT TO YOU ABOUT ACHIEVING THE IDEAL YOU?

WHAT IS IMPORTANT TO YOU ABOUT BECOMING
A SUCCESSFUL REAL ESTATE INVESTOR?

> MAKE MORE MONEY

WHY IS IT IMPORTANT FOR YOU TO MAKE
MORE MONEY?

> GET OUT OF DEBT

WHY IS IT IMPORTANT FOR YOU TO GET
OUT OF DEBT?

> STOP WORKING SO HARD
> TO PAY SOMEONE ELSE

WHY IS IT IMPORTANT FOR YOU TO
STOP WORKING?

> BECAUSE I WANT TO DO
> THINGS IN MY LIFE WITH THE
> FRUITS OF MY LABOUR

WHY IS IT IMPORTANT FOR YOU
TO DO THINGS IN YOUR... ?

> TO TAKE CARE OF MY
> MOTHER WHO IS WIDOWED
> AND NEEDS HELP

SPECIFICALLY, WHY IS IT
IMPORTANT FOR YOU TO
TAKE CARE OF... ?

> BECAUSE SHE SACRALISED
> EVERYTHING TO SEND ME TO COLLEGE
> AND I WANT TO MAKE SURE SHE IS
> TAKEN CARE OF IN HER GOLDEN YEARS

WHY IS IT IMPORTANT
FOR YOU TO TAKE
CARE OF HER... ?

> BECAUSE I WANT TO BE IN CONTROL OF
> MY LIFE SO I CAN HELP THOSE AROUND
> ME (WHO CAN'T HELP THEMSELVES) KNOW
> THEY ARE PRECIOUS, WORTHY AND LOVED

IN SUMMARY, WHAT IS IMPORTANT TO YOU ABOUT BECOMING A SUCCESSFUL REAL ESTATE
INVESTOR?

THE BIG WHY IS: SO YOU CAN BE IN CONTROL OF YOUR LIFE AND HELP THOSE AROUND YOU
(WHO CAN'T HELP THEMSELVES) KNOW THEY ARE PRECIOUS, WORTHY AND LOVED

It's only really by going within and hearing our inner voice that we can even start to identify what our values, needs and meaningful goals are. The inner voice may be ignored or reasoned away because for many it speaks to the most vulnerable part of our stories or ourselves. It can be scary and on the Show we are very careful that if the guest feels uncomfortable or the interview goes to a negative or difficult place then we will listen but not air that episode.

We will continue the interview to the end as we have a duty and respect for that person, but we will also say to the guest that this may not serve you publicly. And that's okay, we will also offer to redo the interview. The guest may have a realisation, whether on the show or in listening back, they may have found that pothole and they may even have filled it or realised a void in their life.

Power of being heard

The first person we need to listen to is ourselves before we even can try and paint the picture of somebody else's view of life, if you can sort your own voice out first. I used to have two voices in my head – the inner critics, put it that way, because in my experience people do hear voices.

Many people can create the space to go within through meditation. I'll be honest and say, I'm not a huge meditator. I struggle with silence, ironically, and consider now even the wording I've used, I struggle with it. That's telling me, I struggle - do I struggle anyway, the power of words? That's what I have told myself - I struggle with silence. So silence for me is not currently my normal state and I have to choose to give myself a bit of space in order to listen to my own voice first. I have learned however that I also benefit and that I can hold that space for somebody else where they can hear their inner voice and voice it.

As host I get to ask a question and reflect their reaction. I can either continue on this thread and keep pulling, pulling, pulling, pulling or let them continue their conversation as it flows for them. I try to do the latter as much as possible however when you give somebody that positive space and ask the next most obvious question you connect. That's not in a false sense. I genuinely am trying to be able to understand and ask the next best question. By the time they've given me all the facts, well now, all of a sudden they have a canvas and can see their beliefs, their expectations and the bigger picture in their lives. Often they will say either on or after the show; 'I had never seen that before.' Or ' That's amazing to me.' As host I have a half finished painting and I've told them nothing, you know, but I've given them the space to hear.

There are a number of tools for going within that may help you to her your inner voice and start to identify your intuition, including choosing to come on as a guest on the show at MightyPete.com/podcast

Here are 5 tools to support you to go within and listen to your inner voice:

1. Complete the top Fire In The Belly Questions and identify your answers to some of the big questions!

2. Do the 7 Levels Deep Exercise contained within this chapter to find your Why?

3. Question things in general, ask yourself why you are doing something, how you feel about it and most of all what you want, really want?

4. Consider sessions of hypnotherapy.

5. Find a mentor and join Mighty Pete for your Fire In The Belly Life Story Talk!

Chapter Ten

Forming the Habits of Hearing

'The first duty of love is to listen.'
- **Paul Tillich**

The power of listening can be heightened and harnessed to that we can hear our way to riches by exploring, learning and both forming and using the habits of hearing. In terms of being a listener as show host I do and I don't have a lot of experience. What I do have are a lot of recent habits that I have formed. When we consider and ask *how do you hear, how do you listen?* I think we need to go further back than that and ask ourselves - *what is listening? Why would we listen?*

'Listening is an art that requires attention over talent,
spirit over ego, others over self.'

- **Dean Jackson**

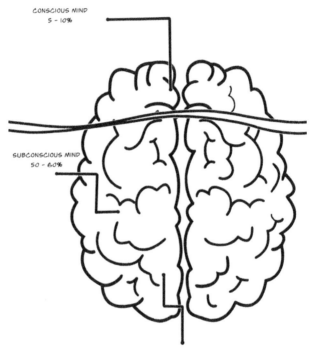

CONSCIOUS MIND
5 – 10%

SUBCONSCIOUS MIND
50 – 60%

UNCONSCIOUS MIND
30–40%

What are we hearing? What are we listening to?

A lot of the time we are hearing background noise. You may or may not be consciously aware of the noise, this type of listening is usually on an unconscious level. It can also be noise that is slightly outside of our frequency, or we might not be aware of it. Research on brittanica.com revealed that the human body sends 11 million bits of information per second to the brain for processing, yet the conscious mind seems to be able to process only 50 bits per second. This tells us that we have a lot of background noise that will stay background noise, unless it is something we recognise.

One of the most therapeutic things for a child is to listen to 'white noise.' They have been in a womb where everything is white noise and it's been described as like listening to the world through a pair of ear muffs. When a child, or any of us, hear a loud noise or a bang or something unusual, it scares us and they go from that unconscious listening to the conscious because something has happened. We often see it in people when we are in a highly populated area with a lot of traffic noise, as long as it stays within the expected pattern and frequency, we can ignore it; we are aware of it somewhere subconsciously but if it changes we instantly become consciously aware and look for the pattern, danger or to identify the reason for the change. It's like a mother would say the kids are playing away but you're listening in the background ... until it's too quiet. It's the same when we overhear a conversation and start to listen because it has pricked our attention and is of interest or inspiration.

In the field of engineering we have to filter information all of the time. We identify and accept that we can't possibly manage all the information being given to us, but we can profile it and establish that if 95% to 98% of the information coming at us is within design tolerances then let's worry about the bit that's not. We choose to hear the 2% or 5% that sit outside the design tolerances then because of our resource limitation, we can then say let's look at the problem. But you've really come to the point where you're making a choice at that stage. You're consciously choosing to listen, even if you've just tuned in for a moment.

In choosing what to show to the world we normally post our best photos and are selective in the news that we share, in recent times however have you noticed that there seems to be an increasing theme of people choosing purposely to post the ugly photo, or their failure of the day and out rightly saying that this is a photo I normally wouldn't show or here's something that happens to me.

Listening as a sense is a form of feeling that is not just about the ears, the two lugs in the side of your head. Hearing ourselves or another is a feeling that is all of our senses wrapped up together; alongside our experiences, knowledge, perception and intuition. In my experience being able to hear is a sense. If we consider people on the African plains or in the desserts where they actively listen for water; they're listening for animal feet or reptiles and insects. Listening is the ability to take on information and filter it in terms of what meaning it has for is, for example; *is this a threat? Is this a friend? Is this a joke? Is this funny? Is this not? Is this something I need to do? Am I reacting? Am I not?*

Hearing and being heard is more than passive noise within the context of this book, it is that most important thing in communication because the quality of our connections and relationships depends on the quality of our communications. The influential business and management consultant Peter Drucker said;

'The most important thing in communication is to hear what isn't being said.'

- **Peter Drucker**

That is to ask; 'where are they looking? Do they look comfortable? Are they engaged and making eye contact? Are they showing that they are listening through language or body language and gesture? Do they look interested or bored? Where are their feet pointing? (not so easy on a podcast)

The potential issues when it coming to hearing ourselves or another is not normally a lack of information. Humans are at a point where we are planning and storing is terms of mega data. Google now has billions of sites and references. So the problem is not information. The problem is getting attention. When we post a picture that I wouldn't normally post, straightaway that's recognised by others as unusual, different to normal and that can get our attention. In this case we're listening by exception.

A lot of people in marketing use selling messages that talk to people's fears? Why? Because people are typically 80% pain driven, 20% pleasure driven and the easiest way to sell to somebody is through pain. You will have seen the posts especially around New Year - are you afraid of getting stuck? Are you afraid of, never achieving your potential? Are you terrified? For many people the answer is yes and they next ask, 'Can you help me?'

On the other hand we see pleasure driven marketing with many of the luxury brands, beauty, travel and lifestyle marketing is normally focussed on communicating luxury, pleasure and a sense of reward.

Why is it powerful when I'm listened to and heard?

Even in the most basic form because we are being bombarded with so much information we often don't know any more *what's my voice? What do I think, what do I feel?* We've often been bombarded with this information over and over again - what's good, what's bad, religion, choice, marketing, food - even school, be a good girl, be a good boy. That's, that's naughty. That's good, that's bad. The power comes in listening and asking ourselves and answering - what do I want? People repeatedly say but it's so hard.

I speak from first-hand experience of knowing that I have to almost zone out everything and go, *what do I actually want? How do I feel about this? And that's not an ego choice – it is saying, right, if I were to wipe the slate clean; What is it, what is my choice? What am I choosing here?* And then test and review.

The 10 Habits of Hearing

1. **The Q & A,** the questions and actions. Ask a question, allow the answer to come to you or hear the answer from another and then immediately put it into action.

2. **Check for understanding.** When you hear the answer to your question, check that you have heard it correctly, say it back and reframe it to yourself or the other. Ask – is this what that means?

3. **Test and Review** and then you've got to ask the question again - does that feel the way I thought it would feel? Is this good for me?

4. **Voids or values?** One of my favourite sayings is 'your voids are your values.' These are set out by Dr John Demartini in his Demartini Value Determination Process. It is an important habit - consider how often do people seek a goal because it's something they didn't have when they were a kid or due to a lack of money, resources or some other previous lack? For example; when people have experienced a lack of money, people may become very money driven. If they're fortunate enough, have a money goal as a focus and they get to the point of having money they will often find that the money means nothing to them. They find that the money is a bit like a hole in the road. The tarmac is coming and they have filled the void and let go of the money goal but it doesn't meet their real values. It was a void, a gap in their life but

then, hold on, what was your original question? *Why am I here?
What's my purpose?*

5. **What is being communicated?** I'm not necessarily listening to
   what guests are saying but I'm trying to hear what they're
   communicating. Consider the language they are actually using or
   that you are using with yourself. Ask questions and watch for
   where they are animated, excited or passionate – it could be their
   kids, the dog, going fishing or whatever. Watch for where they are
   leaning forward.

6. **Listen to how you are feeling.** I have been learning to
   intuitively listen when I am speaking or when I am hearing
   another and I can now identify if I felt a little bit of weird when
   something is said. And now rather than let it go I will take the
   time to pick up on it. I will ask a guest on the show for their
   permission to explore it further and to ask the question. I have
   found that is when people will often say; 'do you know, it's so
   funny you say that.' I understand now that it's not funny at all. It's
   intuitive. It's that the unconscious mind has processed all that
   information and I've listened to identify, *what's the question here?
   What are they getting out? Or what, what are they not getting at?
   Or what are they not saying?*

7. **Check in.** This is to reinforce point 6 - There's a great lesson for
   us when we are able to listen to that feeling of intuition, the 'funny
   feeling' and check in. What a difference that could potentially
   make in terms of our understanding of someone else and our
   understanding of what the issue actually is. If there's a problem, it

might help us to solve it quicker. It's a great lesson to be able to stop with that, feel it and be able to open up and often people will say; 'I'm glad you said that.'

8. **Find your why?** Complete the 7 Levels Deep Exercise contained within this book and regularly. Keep on checking- what is my purpose? You have to ask yourself, am I doing this for me? Am I doing this from being pain driven or pleasure driven? Consider the things that really bring you joy. This is the point where you can get out of the slipstream and that can feel turbulent for a little while as you cross from pain to pleasure. You're going to have a period there of going, oh boy, and suddenly you realise 'I'm on my own! It's up to me.' And that's okay.

9. **Hear your Inner Voice.** Guests on the show will often talk about their inner voice in a number of different ways, as a point of knowing, an actual voice or voices, a gut instinct or intuition. The inner voice for me, and I have learned that it's similar for a few people, is super quiet and it doesn't repeat itself. In order to hear it I need to be listening, to catch it and remember I have to write it down or make a voice note. It is in taking the time to quietly listen and remove all distractions.

10. **Sensory overload.** This can be a useful tool at times of vulnerability or overwhelm. We will hear people say they like to put on trance music or turn music up very loudly so that they almost can't think. When we're in an environment of sensory overload we may arrive at a point of quiet vulnerability because we're communicating directly with the subconscious mind, our

conscious chimp is just chucking a bunch of bananas from the corner, it's given up because it can't keep up. This is the point at which we must allow ourselves or the other person to just listen. On the show it's a point when it would be very easy to insert suggestions but that would not be appropriate - it's a moment of openness and that has to be treated exceptionally respectively.

In creating time and space to hear ourselves or another it is important to set protected time that will not be disturbed. It is the way to make life-changing connections. When you make time to really hear another it is a form of love and creates connection. People feel connected to you and often you will know a lot more about them than potentially their partners or others around them because simply they've never taken the time to do that before and that's not disrespectful, it's the fact that many of us don't know or haven't experienced the impact of being heard in this way before. In an hour and a half to two hours of just hearing another we can learn more about that person than you could potentially do in a lifetime. It is in creating space and being there to actively listen; through the ears and to their perceptions, reflections, body language, intuition, the use of words and their tone.

It is useful to recognise that we all have our potholes in life; the things that we're skirting around or find difficult to acknowledge. It may be that we are completely unaware of what those voids or potholes are. What we can do is identify our values again through completing the exercises throughout this book. A problem can be revealed when our voids meet with somebody else's potholes, having a conversation can be good, but understanding is made possible when an agreement is made for one to be listening without judgement and then take turns. This allows you to set aside applying it to your world and experience. It is understanding that you are painting a picture but that you can only have a fraction of the information – that you can never possibly know their experience as a child or significant events in their life. In setting aside judgement and what it means for you are able to listen without the need for your assumptions or opinions and that allows you to only ask the next most relevant question.

In this way you can Hear your way to Riches.

Being Heard is the path to Being Rich. In this context your 'Being' is your inner most true self that is selfishly complete and is the moral compass by which you are guided. It is this inner most true self that needs to be heard. Remember the word rich can mean the material trappings of life but throughout this book I am referring to the seeds of love, joy, opportunity and potential within every one of us.

Through the chapters and exercises we have explored how to hear and be heard if you want to be rich in life, deepen your connections, create success, build wealth, and find joy, love, peace of mind and happiness.

My intention in sharing the learnings from the Fire In The Belly show is that whatever you are looking for, you will see the benefits in taking the time to listen to your inner genius. In learning how to hear ourselves and others we are moving forward on our life's journey and our soul's purpose of finding itself.

Find your Fire In The Belly.

Be Heard to Be Rich

Reflections from
Fire In The Belly Guests

Connection, wealth, success, love, joy, peace and happiness - what being heard and being rich means for a selection of the guests on the show....

To be heard!

By Pat Slattery

We all have a basic human need to connect. Rather than becoming stuck in the helplessness of a past painful moment or feeling. Keep in mind that there is a future. One that holds potential for you and others.

For some time, I have worked with people that have a desire for growth or for change of some sort. My experience is that the need to listen and to be listened to draws from and cultivates certain capacities. Most people feel the need to feel a part of a conversation with others.

The Fire in the belly podcast is something that I see helps people to find a way to connect with others.

My experience while being interviewed on the podcast is that Pete's way of questioning allows many guests, including myself, to be better able to talk about what is going on inside themselves and in their worlds.

My experience personally, and one that I believe I have seen for other interviewees, is that their capacity to take in and grasp what is being communicated seems to have expanded and deepened.

A new level of sensibility is developing, generating an even deeper understanding and sense of connection.

We human beings are adaptive creatures.

When deprived of our usual ways of meaningfully engaging with others, we find a way. Fire In The Belly is showing the way, it is playing a huge part in allowing people to open up and connect just by simply listening.

People are becoming isolated but the Fire In The Belly podcast is encouraging them to discover and pursue their own ways.

Listen and you will hear, you will feel and you will see!

Pat Slattery is an internationally renowned Mentor, Speaker, Founder of The Outstanding Network and bestselling author.

Connect with Pat at PatSlattery.com

Facebook: Pat Slattery

Facebook: The Outstanding Network

Insta: @slattery.pat

LinkedIn: Pat Slattery

The Silence

By Donna Kennedy

In dictionary terms to listen or hear is 'to give one's attention to a sound.' In that respect when someone says something and we hear the words they say, it could be fair to say that we have heard or listened to them, right? If only!

According to Albert Mehrabian, professor of psychology and author of *The Silent Message,* effective and meaningful communication, is made up of three parts (words account for just 7% of it, tone of voice accounts for 38%, and facial expression for 55%,) all of which need to support each other and be 'congruent', for a message to be fully understood. So, what someone verbally says doesn't necessarily encapsulate what is meant.

What's more, given the fact we live in such a fast-paced world full of distractions and information overload, our chances of actually *hearing* and *understanding* a message when it is verbalised is very much hit and miss.

Most people now listen to respond, not receive. They hover over words being said, picking up bits and pieces along the way, half-listening or sometimes thinking of other things until they resonate with an opportunity to add their bit; their opinions, advice, solutions, and thoughts. The loudness of that anticipated response can often silence what a person cannot convey in words.

And the concerning bit is that depending on what's being said, what's happening at the time (in today's world there is always something happening!) and how interested the 'listener' is in what's being said, the person trying to convey the message has between 8 and 12 seconds to do it, according to various studies on task dependent attention span.

In my opinion, humans have become used to speed and a need for having everything now. It can be frustrating to wait, tedious to learn or explore, and our patience and tolerance for silent gaps is minimal. As a society we have been conditioned to get everything now and fast. So, if someone is trying to get a message across and the listener hasn't the capacity to receive it in that moment, or indeed the person trying to convey the message cannot articulate it well enough or fast enough for the listener, the message can be easily lost, and frustration ensues. What is not expressed is depressed.

If we are to truly hear what people are saying, it is now a matter of consciously slowing down and being open enough to register what is being said in its entirety, not just responding. It is about giving people a chance and becoming comfortable with the silence that precedes expression. Try it for yourself the next time you have a conversation. Note that if nothing is said for 8 seconds or more, (a notable silence), either you or the person you are with will feel compelled to break the 'awkward silence'. Yes, silence has actually become an awkward state. Is silence bad? Of course not, et it's avoided at all costs by many.

I wonder what it would be like if we got comfortable with silences in conversation, for in my experience the silence is often where the key message is. We must acknowledge it without being forceful or hasty. Allow the person to BE in that silence they may feel open to honest expression. Extend the silence and you can hear. *Will you?*

Donna Kennedy (BA Psych (Hons), MHGC, MNLP) is a 7 times bestselling author, psychologist, mentor and highly sought after professional speaker.

Connect with Donna at DonnaKennedy.com

Facebook: Donna Kennedy

Insta: @donnakennedy_com

LinkedIn: Donna Kennedy

Sharing voices and visons

By Louisa Burnett

As an artist my work is about communication and connecting; sharing my voice, my thoughts, and my visions - often with people I do not know and may not ever meet. I want my audience to be captivated by the things I am saying through my work. Partly my need to feel that my work has been validated, because people 'like' it, but also there is a sense of satisfaction knowing people understand and value my way of seeing and creating - and what a driving force that can be.

Other people really do have the power to unlock potential; I have been lucky enough to be surrounded by people who have supported me and believed in me, who have embraced my ideas and that is gold. Simply speaking, talent alone is not enough, that said, I have never been one to wait around for a 'eureka' moment and I have bounced off other people's enthusiasm for what I do.

I will be completely honest, the idea of 'putting myself out there' is something that I have at times found a struggle. I sit somewhere between an introvert and an extrovert, apparently the term is 'ambivert', I can fall into both categories in different circumstances; for the introvert in me, putting myself into the spotlight feels entirely unnatural and completely uncomfortable, whereas the extrovert in me wants to get out there and bask in a blaze of glory.

Whilst we are all capable of being visionary's, dreamers, innovators (and these are the things that give us a head start) if we really have a drive to experience success it's a case of go bold or go home. No room for procrastinating, feeling overwhelmed, feeling scared of failing, but who am I kidding I have done all of the above, many times over, but from experience I know that the shift happens when you strip back those negative tendencies.

Life is strange, it presents opportunities at random times, often when you least expect them and you have to be ready to go with it. Every experience, every encounter, every time you get to share your passion and your voice for whatever it is that you do is step nearer to succeeding.

Louisa Burnett has a background in Fine Art and is an acclaimed artist with her creative arts embracing Painting, Drawing, Illustration and Photography.

Connect with Louisa at:

Facebook: Lula Victoria

Insta: @lula_art6; @lulajewellery, @lulaphotography6

The Power of Positive Reflection

By Paul Coghlan

I consider myself extremely lucky to have been given the opportunity to reflect on my life after a particularly challenging period. I also consider myself extremely lucky to have had the good fortune to meet the outstanding Pete Lonton and to be a guest on his Fire In The Belly podcast series in 2020. It genuinely was an amazing experience.

Having faced a shocking cancer diagnosis in 2018, I made a promise to myself that should I survive against the odds (I was given less than 10%) I would share my story to help as many people as possible that have also been impacted by cancer. For me, reflection is an incredibly powerful tool that helps me to remain positive when I face adversity.

Reflection allows you to process and understand your experiences and to learn important lessons from any challenge you may face. Reflection is a way to help you uncover parts of yourself that you never knew existed and to continuously develop and grow. Reflecting on difficult challenges can bring you on a pretty intense emotional rollercoaster. There is uncertainty, frustration, anger and disappointment. But with a shift in perspective, there is also HOPE, and it is on this positive note that I will share some insights on what I have learned through positive reflection.

I have learned that everybody needs to be aware of their internal chatter in order to reflect and grow in a positive way. Try to talk to yourself as you would to a dear friend. Navigating your way through any challenge is a time to aim for progress and not perfection. Remember that reflection is an ongoing personal project and you will not master I overnight. You need to become more aware of being self-critical and aim to practice positive self-talk every day. Remember the only person you are in a relationship with for your entire life is you! The person you speak to the most each day is yourself.

I have learned to adapt to change with more grace. Accepting any change that isn't wanted is often an unexpected part of life that we all face at some point. Change is difficult, but being aware of what is within your control will help you to prioritize what you should focus your attention on. Instead of focusing on what you cannot do, focus on what you can do.

I have learned to focus on the good. When you feel overwhelmed, take a step back and look at the many aspects of your life that bring you joy and make you smile. You have a choice. You can train your brain to look for the negative things every day or the positive things every day. Practise appreciation and happiness and see your life in a more positive way. This exercise involves noting all the positive things that happened to you during or at the end of each day, thereby focusing on the good and positive moments in every day.

I have learned to surround myself with a team of cheerleaders. Encouragement is the action of instilling courage into someone through the provision of support, confidence and hope. Life is not always easy. Some days are harder than others but having the right people around you can make a huge difference. Make a conscious choice of who you select to have around you.

Remember that you are your own best friend and it is always important to look after your own wellness. Self-care is the most beautiful gift you can give yourself. This is about prioritising time for yourself and doing the little things that make life about you, even for just a few moments each day. Self-care does not have to take hours or cost a fortune. Your time out might just be a quiet cup of coffee, a sit down with a cosy blanket, a walk and talk, gardening, a meal out with your loved ones...etc. It is about deciding that you are important enough to make time for yourself to do something that you love.

If, after reading this you feel like you need to change or improve any part of your life, remember that reflection is often not straight forward. This is your journey and its pace will be unique and individual to you. Find a pace that works for you and make small improvements regularly.

Before you can 'be Heard to be rich,' you first need top people around you to get your message across, to carve out and fine tune your idea and dare I say, uncover one's genius. Working with Pete has been incredibly helpful with fulfilling my voice, sharing my story and greatly aiding me in bringing it to others. His expert authentic approach put me at ease and allowed me to be calm, comfortable and confident while sharing lessons and insights from my journey with leukaemia. The incredible feedback I received was testament to the man, his podcast and his belief in himself and others.

I am now pushing forward with clarity and confidence. An online course that brings my story of adversity to light with the solid goal of sharing the lessons cancer has taught me to help and enrich the lives of others who are beginning their journey with adversity.

To be heard can enrich and save a life so this book is very aptly named.

Paul Coghlan is a Motivational Speaker and the founder of What I Learned From Cancer. Paul is on a personal journey to share what he has learned from facing cancer.

Connect with Paul at PaulCoghlan.ie

Facebook: Paul Coghlan Motivational Speaker

Insta: @paulcoghlan78

LinkedIn: Paul Coghlan Motivational Speaker

Talking to Think

By Lisa Stevenson

When you talk to someone, do you feel you are actually being heard? Or are you just being listened to and they are going through the usual reactions of your conversation while they are thinking about their own tasks they have to face today?

Being on 'Fire In The Belly' podcast I definitely know I was being heard when Pete asked questions in relation to what I was saying that really made me think on a different level. It was like a breath of fresh air. Pete has a unique skill in the way he communicates with you and I have to say he is amazing.

I am quite a shy and reserved person who doesn't enjoy talking in public and certainly not about myself and my successes. He put me at ease right from the start and I was able to speak more openly and honestly than I think I ever have and felt safe in the process forgetting (thankfully) that there would be so many people being able to listen to my story – who would want to hear my story after all? He asked me questions that made me think in a way I have never done before and in the process I was able to remember things that I haven't thought of in a very long time, able to see and understand things in a different light and had some powerful ah-ha take away moments too!

Talking to someone like Pete definitely makes you think more deeply and he helps you to find more clarity and understanding – even in things that you may think you already are clear in and understand well already.

The next time you are talking to someone try to listen to what they are saying, not what you think they are saying because you have 101 things going on in your head already – you could be surprised with what you hear and what you may learn from doing it.

All too often we may think we are listening and understanding but the question is, are we? Can we listen and understand more?

Deep inside all of us, YES all of us, there is an inner genius that we may be suffocating, unconsciously perhaps, and it really wants to come out and help you grow and succeed. All it needs is for someone to encourage it to come out by asking a few different questions that may make you think in a different way and give you the belief that YOU CAN do more and be more than what you are doing now. What is your inner genius trying to tell you? I would truly love to know.

My Fire in the Belly is helping people; physically, emotionally and/or spiritually by providing holistic treatments, meditations or via my Happy Minds journals that I have produced for kids (and soon to be for teens and adults too) to help them lead a more positive, happy and calm life.

After nearly 20 years of working as an adult nurse where I helped hundreds, if not thousands of people, during particular journeys of their lives I knew when I made the decision to leaving the nursing profession that I still wanted to help people in any way I could, to help them to heal themselves and help to make their lives more peaceful and fulfilling. The gratitude that I feel receiving messages from people from all over the world when they tell me how their kids are loving their journals and how much happier they are is amazing! Seeing my clients leave me after a treatment with a bounce in their step, looking less stressed, feeling amazing and seeing their symptoms resolving over time is extremely rewarding too! I love seeing people relax and enjoy life as much as they can and being part of that process is amazing! What do you love doing? Have you found the fire in your belly yet?

Lisa Stevenson is a highly inspiring and successful holistic therapist, meditation teacher, author of My Happy Mind Activity Journals, founder of Think Calm Be Calm and owner at Pamper and Relax Beauty Salon.

Connect with Lisa at ThinkCalmBeCalm.co.uk

Facebook: Lisa Stevenson

Facebook: Think Calm Be Calm

Facebook: Pamper and Relax

Insta: @lisastevenson81, @pamperrelax, @thinkcalmbecalm

LinkedIn: Lisa Stevenson

The me that was and the me that is

By Mary Keogh

The Me that was...The lost, frightened, insecure little girl that I connect with as I begin to write, she just pops right out at me and now she is going to tell her story.

Do you see me? I am here just look at me, I feel so alone in this tiny little body. Can you hear my little voice? It's pleading to be heard, yet in my tiny little world no-one sees me no one hears me.

Loud voices - adults exchanging words that seem to be wrong and I feel an uneasiness taking hold of me, my body becomes jelly like and I sense something is wrong. I do not want to listen, so I go to the corner in my room where I huddle down and wait for it to end.

Silence falls but it's not a safe silence 'oh please just let everyone be friends' I hear my tiny little voice whisper.

I rock back and forward waiting for someone to come to pick me up and tell me everything is ok, but no-one comes.

My little voice becomes my constant companion it listens to all that is going on around me and it then tells me what to do, how to think and behave. My little voice never tells me anything nice it's always telling me that I am not good enough and no one cares about me and everything is my fault that if I were different then my home would be different. My little me voice has now created for me how I see myself, how I value myself and how much I dislike myself.

As I grew my little voice came with me and I now had grown into an adult body as a broken child; my emotions and feelings had not changed because I was still re-enacting daily the habits and behaviours of a broken child - the language in my head had never changed and my guidance in life was that of a broken child –THAT WAS ME.

Nothing took away the deep desperation to be loved and accepted, it was a constant ache in my heart. Life didn't shine for me, it was just there, I accepted what life threw at me because after all who was I but the adult of a broken child, so I tried to be all things to everybody and pleasing everyone in my life and the more I did the more I was lost.

I attracted people and situations into my life that took and never gave but I believed that was ok because at least there were people in my life – well, that is what the broken child kept telling me.

Life began to smother me. I struggled to breath in a world where my biggest influencer was ME the broken child. I had run out of steam and the train was leaving without me unless I got rid of the unnecessary baggage that was holding me down and yet this baggage was all I had, all I knew and I hadn't a clue who I was, death looked kinder - an easier option, but I didn't have the courage to carry it through.

So, ME the broken child and the adult broken child made one of the biggest decisions in our lives and that was to heal the broken child. I began to unpack the unhealthy baggage of a lifetime and in that process, I became vulnerable and raw but, in this space, I began to heal the broken child that was ME.

I nurtured her, I forgave her, I embraced her, and I loved her back to a place where she now journeys with me daily in my soulful heart, she is part of who I am but she now rests in her childlike place.

Once I healed 'THE ME THAT WAS' - 'THE WOMAN THAT IS' was waiting to make an appearance and there she was looking back at me in a mirror, that me who was waiting for the breakthrough, who was waiting to present herself once I could let go of the me that was.

There looking back at me – she had all my answers and was not interested in how my hair looked or how I dressed; it was good to look well but she was an inner spirit who wanted to take my hand and take me on a journey of self-belief, self-worth and self-love.

I opened my whole self-up to this inner self and I found that I began to value who I was, I respected the woman I was becoming and I put boundaries in place whereby all that I was becoming was a sacred space and the only other voice I listened to was the inner spirit who loved me back to life, who nursed me when I struggled and who danced with me when I found true happiness within myself. Yes, I found my true soulmate looking back at me in the mirror; the genius that I am has now presented itself to a universe that has unfolded inner gifts beyond my wildest dream. The genius in me does not fly solo anymore because I fly with my copilot. My journey is now one where I grace people with an inner healing and guide them on a path to find their true self.

In the healing of the broken child and the birthing of my true self I had the privilege of been a guest on Fire in my Belly.

During this very in depth and personal conversation I was given the space to enter a place where I discovered my true purpose. I know that Pete Lonton helped unravel in me what my true calling was and it was a moment that I sat in true grace.

In the silence of all that I am, I open my true self to that silence where my soul speaks to me. I am learning to trust the safety of this space and in doing so I listen for my answers. In the silence is found my universe.

What I have been given is priceless; money could never buy the soulmate, inner genius and 'THE ME THAT IS '

In grace I stand.

Your Mary Godmother x

Mary Keogh a.k.a Your Mary Godmother is an acclaimed coach and founder of the Mary Keogh Life Mastery Academy which specialises in personal development, group coaching, life management coaching, parenting seminars and health and wellbeing.

Connect with Mary at MaryKeogh.co.uk

Facebook: Mary Keogh

Insta: @mary_keogh

LinkedIn: Mary Keogh

Into Your Being's Depth

By Linda Carmichael

Pete's 6 foot something friendly appearance may fool you into thinking being a guest on his podcast 'Fire in the Belly' will be a breeze; a friendly chat if nothing else and for that I can forgive you. You would be mistaken. It's more than just an interview on what you feel is your passion; it's a journey into your being's depth.

The question, 'Is anything off-limits?' may consciously prepare you to be a little guarded with your words, but I can assure you it's a battle you will lose most beautifully!

I had a wonderful experience of realising my childhood was incredible when I took the time to analyse it, rather than only focusing on the bad or the ugly. After the interview, I felt more grateful than ever for what I had and the family relationships I misjudged as an adult.

It would have been hard to miss the emotion and joy on my face when I spoke about the people I valued in my life the most, both past and present and that's a gift not everyone enjoys.

All served with a healthy side of vulnerability, making his podcast not just an opportunity to claim who you are but release the fire in your belly!

Linda Carmichael is a highly successful global business owner and founder of Make Me Mold Me where she creates high quality silicone molds designed for resin jewellery making. Linda is also a Handmade Business Mentor.

Connect with Linda at her Etsy Store Make Me Mold Me

Facebook: Make Me Mold Me

Insta: @makeme_moldme

LinkedIn: Linda Carmichael

The Other Side Of The Mic

By Camilla Long

Being a guest on the Fire in the Belly show has been transformational for me. And not for the reasons you might think! From following the show I already knew that Pete has the gift of asking meaningful questions that go deep. I was thrilled when I was invited on as a guest. But when it came to my turn to sit on the other side of the mic, the experience made me feel very vulnerable. In fact I was surprised to realise just how uncomfortable I felt.

So after the interview I needed to question where that feeling came from and this reflection began a journey of self-discovery that has changed so much in my life in a few short months. I've gone and set new audacious life goals that I never would otherwise have considered. I have developed stronger relationships with my kids. I have attracted new clients to my business. My interview had the unintended consequence of forcing me to open my mind to new possibilities.

And the interesting part about all of this is that I'm no stranger to being interviewed, on stage or on radio. I am a public speaking coach, so I'm used to talking about myself! I work with people to become more visible and build their influence in the networks that matter to them. Part of that journey to influence is the willingness to be vulnerable.

Vulnerability is different for everyone – for some it's the willingness to let people in and reveal who they really are, for others it's making the decision to stand up in front of an audience that terrifies them. For those in visible leadership positions, vulnerability can mean standing up in a public forum and taking accountability for their actions. Because that's what builds connections, as hard and as challenging as it may be.

As an introvert, I feel the need to hide away from some behaviours that don't come naturally. I will never be the one with the funniest joke, the sharpest analysis or the quickest response. And when I drilled down, it was that fear of being found out that made me so uncomfortable in this open interview format. But I am enough. I have the ability to see the greatness in others. And by being my words, I can draw the very best out of those around me. That is my Fire in the Belly.

Camilla Long is the co-founder of Bespoke Communications and is an expert in communications, powerful presentation, public speaking coach and event host.

Connect with Camilla at BespokeComms.net

Facebook: Bespoke Communications

Insta: @bespokecomms

LinkedIn: Bespoke Communications, Camilla Long

Inner Game and Outer Game

By Alexander Inchbald

Truly hearing, seeing or feeling someone is very rare. I'm not talking about hearing their voice or seeing their body. I'm talking about hearing and seeing the whole person: both what I call the Inner Game and the Outer Game, the feminine and the masculine, the shadow and the light, what we want to see, hear and feel and what we don't want to see, hear and feel. This is rare, because in order to do this, we need to see, hear and feel the entirety of ourselves. And yet, this is Mighty Pete's intention with Fire in the Belly.

So, what is our Inner Game and our Outer Game? Here's how I described it in my latest bestselling book, #Masterpiece - what you would do with all the time and money in the world :

'Every cultural tradition describes a duality that exists inside us. Most of us flip-flop between these worlds without a consistently balanced mindset that links them: psychologists talk about the conscious and the unconscious; philosophers talk about the personality and the essence; artists talk about the intellect and intuition; and scientists talk about the Newtonian physical world of things and the Einsteinian metaphysical world of ideas.'

I call it the Inner Game and Outer Game, based on Bob Anderson and Bill Adam's research in their book Mastering Leadership. Their research with over 250,000 leaders around the world found that those who lead with their Inner Game are up to 1,000 times more effective than those who don't.

Even if we understand this, most of us still use our Outer Game to tackle the symptoms of the problems we face... we can see these symptoms at a societal, organizational and personal level: we have the highest temperatures and record levels of inequality, debt, natural disasters, ecological destruction, unemployment, distrust, disengagement, divorce, depression, sleep deprivation, poor diet and addiction. Is it a coincidence we see all of these symptoms at the same time? I think not. Everything is connected.

'Pollution is not outside us. Pollution is inside us.'

— Thich Nhat Hanh

The Outer Game

Ever since the agricultural revolution [around 10,000 years ago], we have increasingly been using The Outer Game to tackle these challenges. So, what is the Outer Game? It consists of our identity or personality. The doorway into the Outer Game is our first five senses: our sight, hearing, touch, taste and smell. This is how we connect to the world outside us. The key to unlock our Outer Game is our strengths. We can use psychological profiling tools like Myers Briggs Type Indicator (MBTI), Gallup StrengthsFinder, Wealth Dynamics from GeniusU (the largest community of entrepreneurs in the world) to identify our strengths.

Your Outer Game creates influence.

I have developed my own tool, called The Artist Profile which explains how each of us creates in one of four different ways. All of these tools are based on the same Source—the I Ching, or the Book of Changes, a 5,000-year-old book from China. When we unlock our Outer Game, we unlock our ability to influence our world by bringing our Masterpiece to life.

The Inner Game

So what is the Inner Game? The Inner Game is much harder to describe. Because as soon as I give it a term, I will trigger your belief system, what you believe about the world—in other words, which paradigm you are primarily operating from, and this is influenced by your culture, your upbringing and your experiences. So, rather than give it a name, I will let you give it a name. What's easier to describe is how you access the Inner Game. The doorway to the Inner Game is your Sixth Sense, your intuition. The key to unlock it is your Personal Purpose. When we unlock our Purpose, we unlock creativity, collaboration, compassion and courage — all the things that we need today in order to tackle the root cause of the symptoms we talked about, whether they be at a societal, organizational or personal level.

Your Inner Game creates connection.

When we align our Outer Game with our Inner Game, by putting our ego and influence at the service of our essence and inner connection, we change our behavior rather than attempting to manipulate the world outside us. We create the fertile conditions in which a Masterpiece can emerge. We are in a state of flow, in the zone and in this moment, we can create miracles.

Miracles and mindset

A few years ago, I ended up painting in a blizzard. I hadn't intended to paint in a blizzard. It just kind of happened. As the snow started to fall more heavily, I started to lose control over the canvas. My ego, my identity, kicked in because the paint was starting to run. But as I started to observe what was happening on the canvas, I started to see something really interesting was occurring. The snow was merging with the paint and creating really interesting patterns.

So, I paused, and stopped painting. I stopped reacting to the snow; stopped resisting it. The palette became covered in so much snow that I could hardly see the paint. But rather than resist, I continued to brush; painting through the snow, rather than against it. I wondered at the time whether it was me, or the snow that was panting the picture. It certainly wasn't my ego. That had dissolved into me. Was it my essence? Or was it something greater? Was the entire ecosystem creating in unity?

I didn't care. All I knew was that I felt at one, in total peace. Towards the end of the painting, I turned to Tony, my friend who had been filming me, and asked him if the painting was finished... At the exact moment he said 'Yes' the sun came out and the snow and ice which had merged with the paint, holding it together, started to melt. Everything dissolved. The paint ran off the canvas, nothing holding it together, leaving me with a blank canvas: the same blank canvas I had started with. And a video to show what happened.

The funniest thing is, in that state, I was happy to let it go. The experience had been so mind-altering for me, I didn't care. When we are in total balance, we are in unity with ourselves and everything around us. We feel safe although we may be doing something that would appear incredibly unsafe.

When our Outer Game merges with our Inner Game, we become part of the ecosystem again. There is no separation. We are at one, in unity, at peace. In the process, we see the world outside us is a blank canvas on which we can create anything we choose. It's always a blank canvas. But because we're so wrapped up in our thoughts we miss this essential truth. That we are the universe and influence everything in it, not just with our actions, but also with our presence. How else can we explain metaphysical phenomena such as healing people without drugs, levitating, talking in tongues, or changing the weather?

'I am Life. I am the space in which all things happen. I am consciousness. I am.'

— Eckhart Tolle

Alexander Inchbald is an Extreme Artist, founder of Create Your Masterpiece, founder Masterpiece Movement, bestselling Author, Coach and founder WorldClass Academy.

Connect with Alexander at Alexander-Inchbald.com

Facebook: Alexander Inchbald Art Is Inside

Insta: @alexander_inchbald

LinkedIn: Alexander Inchbald

Being Heard is Rich for the Soul

By Gary Doherty

I have reflected a lot on being heard and sharing my story on Mighty Pete Lonton's Fire in the Belly podcast. I have shared my story on many forums but this was different. If I was to give you words to describe it, profound, deep and interesting.

I went to places in my mind I had avoided or at the very least not been vocal about. It was a therapeutic for me. I got a weight off my chest and in a positive, safe, constructive, non-judgmental environment. It truly was a great experience for me.

I love the book title and for me be heard to be rich means many things. The two main ones being that being heard is rich for the soul , rich for your emotional and spiritual wellbeing. It frees you internally and empowers you. It did for me. In my own TED Talk at TEDx Cookstown I talk about the fear of public speaking so to have done this was a full 360 degree turn for me. I'm very proud of that.

In addition to that and putting my economic and commercial business hat on. I firmly believe being heard to be rich should be one of the fundamental social media strategies for everyone striving to achieve greatness and success. In my view if you are not visible you are invisible. If you are not being heard no one knows you and no one cares. Business is ruthless and you must be too. Move forward with your integrity and values at your core but with the firm intention of your voice being heard on ALL platforms. Be omni present. Marketing experts will tell you focus on this and that. I am telling yes have a focus but don't miss a trick. Be everywhere!

Gary Doherty is a TEDx Speaker, founder of global empowerment platform Think Network, founder and host TEDxDerry Londonderry, Author and Speaker

Connect with Gary at ThinkNetwork.co

Facebook: Think Network

Facebook: TEDxDerryLondonderry

Insta: @think.network, @tedxderrylondonderry

LinkedIn: Gary Doherty, Think Network, TEDxDerryLondonderry

Live In Absolute Mightiness

By Liam O'Neill

In order to listen to your inner genius, you first must become aware of your inner genius, for most people this happens during their journey of Self-Reflection.

Self-Reflection can and should be done at any time, you do not have to wait until you hit rock bottom before deciding you need to take a good look at yourself, and you can put the brakes on at any time and start the upward journey now.

Self-Reflection is hard but also liberating, when you know your faults and take ownership of them, no one can use them against you. When you know your real core values, how you really want to live your life, who you really are as a person, then no one can take you of your path, in fact you will have the strength of character to stand up for yourself and how you live your life.

Confidence, Self-Belief, Courage and Strength of Will; these all come from Self-Reflection, when you know yourself you are happy to share what you know, in fact you want to share it, you want to be heard, once you feel the benefits of unlocking your true potential, you want everyone to feel that freedom for themselves.

As this question has come from the 'Fire In The Belly' podcast I will use an analogy involving our voice, most 'normal' people, on hearing their own voice through a recording will, wince, shy away or in extreme cases actually throw up a little in their mouth, just from hearing their own voice, the voice they have had most of their lives.

Why does this happen?

Well science tells us that when we speak we hear about 50% of our own voice through bone conduction making our voice sound lower and fuller, but when we hear a recording it is actually traveling through the air making us hear it at a higher, squeaker pitch, meaning the voice we usually hear sounds different to the one you hear on a recording. That's some of the science anyway.

In my experience the reason is, a fear of change, combined with a lack of confidence because we think we cannot deal with change, this all comes from a lack of Self- Reflection.

I find that people are almost afraid to look closely at themselves, they are worried about what they might learn; turns out I am not as happy as I claim I am or I talk about doing charity work and being helpful to the community but I haven't done anything like that in ages.

Basically put, if you avoid looking closely at yourself you can believe anything about yourself you wish.

Self-Reflection forces you to look at yourself, to see your faults, to choose to change them or to choose not to, making you eliminate any excuses you may have.

What has this got to do with the being heard or getting rich for that matter?

The easy answer is, you will never be heard if you don't know the lessons your inner genius wants to teach, and you will never know what your inner genius knows without Self-Reflection.

The longer answer is this, Self-Reflection is an ever changing journey, with lonely paths, dead ends, rickety bridges and all sorts of things in your way, some you will have seen before and understand, others you will have no idea how to traverse. These are the best bits, these are the bits that really teach you who you are, this is where you will find out what you are really made of, what you really want to do and most importantly where you really want to go.

I found myself on an inward journey by mistake, I was lost in life, going with the flow without knowing what direction the river was flowing, I was forced to start meditation which actually opened me up to Self-Reflection, on one of my meditations, my mind just expanded, I found myself at the edge of a cliff, my higher self was already there, seated in a lotus position, looking complete, balanced and calm, I stood quietly looking at myself, watching the stillness, after I don't know how long I finally asked myself a question.

Who am I?

Ask yourself this question and answer with honesty, it may take a minute, an hour, a day or even a year but the answers will change your life.

I believe we can all be anything we want to be.

I believe we all have a story that should be heard.

I believe that if we get out of our own way we can get rich.

I believe that Limitation Is A Mirage.

Liam O'Neill is an acclaimed Hypnotherapist, Life Coach, Podcaster, Mentalist and Author and is known as The 'Prove It' Guy.

Connect with Liam at LimitationIsAMirage.com

Facebook: Liam O'Neill The 'Prove It' Guy

Insta: @theproveitguy

LinkedIn: Liam O'Neill

Hearing Myself through Being Heard

By Heather Shields

When I first realised how far off track that I had become a few years ago I felt very frightened. I had stopped listening to myself, I could no longer hear my intuition and I didn't know what I wanted or where I was going.

I have three wonderful children and had loved my job but somehow the previous seven years had gone by very quickly as I worked, raised my children and helped to care for my grandparents who were living with dementia. I was constantly busy. There was always a child's activity, event, meeting or something to do or attend.

Through all the busyness I took little time to listen to myself. Listen to others - yes, in fact much of my day involved actively listening to others and even educating people on how to actively listen to people affected by dementia in order to better understand what they are communicating as the disease progresses.

But listen to myself?

What would it mean or could it mean if I stopped and took the time to listen? I understand now that this may have been a deliberate coping mechanism at that time in my life.

Change started slowly – I introduced meditation as a way to sleep better, then as a way to sleep less. I found that I could meditate and that it worked for me. Soon I was meditating morning and night and felt a real benefit in both my emotional and spiritual health. I joined a meditation group and made great new friends and expanded my meditation practice.

As I faced a number of big life changes including the death of both my grandparents, just two weeks apart in February 2017, I found that I needed a physical outlet and at 38 years of age joined a gym for the first time, working out three times a week and starting to do weights.

I found my confidence increasing and although my love for my job and appreciation of my great colleagues remained I had an inner knowing that I was changing my life. That it was time for a new direction. I started reading and listening to new things, I found a mentor for the first time and would later join a mastermind; I read Think and Grow Rich by Napoleon Hill, You2 by Price Pritchett and Your Invisible Power by Genevieve Behrend. I re-read The Power of Now by Eckhart Tolle and A Return to Love by Marianne Williamson. I finally did A Course in Miracles. I found The Fire In The Belly show and was a regular listener from the second show – I loved the concept of real people, sharing life stories and the fact that people on the show were reflective, often vulnerable and that I was learning from them. I learned to listen, to listen to my inner voice but I still didn't always trust it.

I would soon have the great privilege of both listening to and being listened to by Mighty Pete on the Fire In The Belly Show. The fact is that when I first appeared on the show in September 2020 we had just recently started to work together as I had been appointed editor for this book, Be Heard To Be Rich. In the journey of writing this book Pete has brought many gifts to me in the process that started when I appeared on the show. It was Pete who first identified my 7 year life cycles and how my life had seemed to change in some form every 7 years. It was also on the show that I would voice my vision and how I wished my life goals to grow and the direction that I was choosing for the next stage in my life.

It was, for me, one of those conversations of a lifetime. And yet it wasn't a conversation but Pete had gently, and with the great awareness that only a world-class mentor can bring, guided me through a conversation with myself.

In that conversation and through asking the next most obvious question I found clarity and through speaking my truth – confidence.

It was a remarkable gift. Thank you Mighty Pete.

Heather Shields is a bestselling Author, Publisher, Editor and Ghost-writer who listens to people's stories and puts them onto paper and into a book ready to publish. Heather is also a Co-founder of The Self-Publishing Network and self-publishing coach.

Connect with Heather at HeatherShieldsPublishing.com

Facebook: Heather Shields

Insta: heather_shields.publishing

LinkedIn: Heather Shields

Listen To Your Inner Genius

By Annie M Henderson

Being truly listened to can be transformational.

So many people might have family, friends and coworkers that physically hear them, but listening is intentional. As a Life Coach, I experience this with my clients on a daily basis. Like most, they are surrounded by everyone and their opinions. But as crab mentality exemplifies, those around us will ultimately hold us back with their own fears involving change and growth. This is why many struggle to grow in our current environment, and reach outside our 'bucket' for motivation, support and a fresh mindset.

Ask yourself, do you have someone in your life that can listen and support?

We cannot solve our problems with the same thinking that created them.

- Albert Einstein

I love being a life coach and seeing the growth when clients are really listened to. Game changer!

The Fire in the Belly Podcast and Pete Lonton are so different in the podcast world.

Pete does an amazing job of truly listening, asking questions and truly holding space to hear the stories behind the answer and **Does. Not. Rush.**

Even after multiple grad degrees, certifications, and coaching and counseling others... Pete still tenderly touched my heart....because he actually listened. That's right! I got choked up on Fire in the Belly!

When I look back and think of everything that our world consumes vs internalises, my jaw drops and I nod with my own reflection. For so much of my life, I consumed books, podcasts, and degrees and jumped from one thing to the next without being able to simply soak it in to a deeper level.

Yes, I could repeat, pass a test, use it to help others. But if you haven't noticed this yet....we have blinders on when it comes to our own lives, decisions, thoughts.

This is one reason that women, after decades of holding themselves back and trying to get to that next level on their own, can shift and grow by leaps and bounds in just months when working with a Life Coach.

This is why counselors, coaches, professional athletes, and CEOs invest in their own future by having a Life Coach.

Life Coaching is for everyone and as a former teacher and school counselor, I wish it was something that everyone got to experience as they grow up. Can you imagine?

Annie Henderson is better known as Life Coach Annie and is a Coming Out Coach, Author, Counselor and leading global Podcaster of both 'The Happy Mama' and 'Coming Out Loved and Supported' Podcasts.

Connect with Annie at AnnieMHenderson.com

Facebook: Annie M Henderson

Insta: @life_coach_annie

LinkedIn: Annie M Henderson, The Coming Out Coach

I am Hungry!

By Danielle Bell

It was an absolute honour to have been asked to appear on The Fire In The Belly podcast, an experience I thoroughly enjoyed - although admittedly I was tentative about it at first.

I have been infamously private my entire life, sharing only what I've deemed necessary and closing down any further probing. To say my interview with Pete turned that on its head would be an understatement.

This guy has a gift for opening the floodgates and bringing down the barriers in the most subtle of ways. My interview on Pete's podcast revealed more to me about myself than I had ever truly acknowledged; it allowed me to really dig deep on what had been holding me back becoming the best version of myself.

The result?

A brand new Danielle left the room that day, an empowered Danielle, an enlightened and energised Danielle, a Danielle who refused to allow the judgment of others to affect creating the life she knew was possible, a HUNGRY MUMMY.

The verdict?

You most certainly do need to BE HEARD TO BE RICH. It was an honour to have been invited on to speak with Pete who I class as a dear friend and a force to be reckoned with in his own right.

Thank you for allowing me to be heard!

Danielle Bell is a leading Property Investor focussed on sharing her learning and creating a community of property investors as founder of Property Sourcing Made Simple with Danielle Bell, founder of Hungry Mummy.

Connect with Danielle at Subscribepage.com/property

Facebook: Property Sourcing Made Simple

Insta: @iamdaniellebellproperty

LinkedIn: Danielle Bell

Nourished

By Cliodhna Fullen

From the moment we are born we express our emotion through crying and shouting and then eventually talking. We scream for attention, food, comfort and love. *Why?* To be heard in all areas of life that will nourish us. To communicate. A trait that never leaves us, a trait that we can struggle to deal with and understand.

Why have we placed so much energy and focus into the importance of being heard? To be heard some might say is a cry for help or attention. However you wish to look at it, there is definitely a reason. Being heard is something humans feel is a fundamental function as doesn't everyone? Don't we all have something worthwhile to say at some point in time?

As a species we have particular unique mental faculties that gives us a very different perception of things. Our perception is what makes us all different and unique. We were not born to be the same but yet we struggle to accept others who are different.

In today' modern world, with a simple click on your phone you can witness almost everything happening in the world, supporters expressing their voices, tragic weather events unfolding, war & famine as well as positive events and support for the human race. While witnessing these from multiple sources and sometimes in real-time, you can have a different option or perspective from everyone else.

The interesting fact about 'being heard' is sometimes people don't want to listen. We are merely awaiting our turn to respond with our voice. The irony is, most of us don't like the sound of our own voice but are determined to make sure it's heard. Somewhere in history we have attached righteousness to our freedom of speech. If we feel we are not heard, some shout louder or perhaps go to extreme lengths to vent their opinions or beliefs. Social movements have originated from this, protests, marches, rallies, cultures shifts and even wars. Our current social media platforms have given us more freedom to voice opinions and make sure they have an outlet for being heard. *Is this the correct strategy? Why is there such a passion within us to be heard? Where did it come from?*

Our perception is 'the sensory experience of the world.' Maybe if we focus more on listening vs speaking, we could potentially hear what's going on deep within us and others - our inner true voice. A voice that we need to be gentle with and can sometimes ignore. A voice so powerful, yet for some consumed with negative self-beliefs. A voice we should be proud of that has taught us many lessons in life if we listened.

I suggest we understand our own voice first, before we listen to another's. Communication is essential, however the most important part of being heard is to first listen to yourself.

Cliodhna Fullen works closely with clients as a Motivational Life Skills Mentor, is a well-known TV presenter / Director and Blogger.

Connect with Cliodhna:

Facebook: Cliodhna Fullen

Facebook: Cliodhna Fullen Blog

Insta: @cliodhnafullen

LinkedIn: Cliodhna Fullen

Acknowledgements

I want to thank everyone who has been a Guest on the Fire In The Belly show, each and every one of you have been a source of learning for me personally and have inspired this book. I have been blessed and honoured to sit with and hear 400 people share their Life Story with me and the listeners.

The Fire In The Belly team are so grateful for all of those who listen to the show and for the insights gained and shared as a result. It is always a point of deep appreciation to receive a thank you note, comment or positive feedback from anyone who has been touched by a Life Story Talk.

In creating this book I would like to thank the following people for their direct contributions, reflections and creative inputs;

Mark Victor Hansen for his much-valued endorsement of Be Heard To Be Rich.

For providing reflections, testimonials and encouragement: Pat Slattery, Donna Kennedy, Mary Keogh, Paul Coghlan, Louisa Burnett, Linda Carmichael, Lisa Stevenson, Camilla Long, Alexander Inchbald, Gary Doherty, Liam O'Neill, Heather Shields, Annie M Henderson and Danielle Bell.

To my Editor Heather Shields for the many interesting conversations as I was developing the themes and, of course, for editing the book.

284 | B e   H e a r d   T o   B e   R i c h

Throughout the book you have met Mighty Mr Stick – a big thank you to Artist Nikita McGonigle for providing all of the illustrations.

For cover and website design: Alan Wallace at All The Way Creative for bringing my vision to life with his unique flair.

Personally, I would like to thank those closest to me including my sister Georgina Lonton, members of my morning reading group and mentors; in particular with regards to this chapter in my life Pat Slattery, Rob Moore and Liam O'Neill for their constant support, enlivening conversations and encouragement. I would also like to thank those that I have the privilege of being a mentor to for being part of my journey and allowing me to journey with them as they follow their fire.

Finally, my greatest thanks is to my wife Julie and our three daughters. The love that I have for them is my why, the love and connection within the family life that we have created together. In the process of writing this book Julie has shown endless patience, guidance and commitment to reading. Thank you Julie.

Thank you to everyone who reads this book – may you hear your way to riches!

Wealth Builder Academy

- ❖ Consider what wealth means to you
- ❖ Learn how to build financial wealth
- ❖ Identify your assets
- ❖ Build your legacy
- ❖ Find out more at MightyPete.com

Property Portfolio Builder

Mighty Pete is a highly successful Property Investor having built up a large portfolio over the past 21 years and is founder of Progressive Property Network Northern Ireland.

You can now learn from Pete's experience through his **90-day Property Portfolio Builder!** Connect with Pete at MightyPete.com

Testimonials for Being Heard on the Fire In The Belly podcast:

'Fire in the belly is showing the way, it is playing a huge part in allowing people to open up and connect just by simply listening.

People are becoming isolated, the Fire In The Belly podcast is encouraging them to discover and pursue their own ways.'

- **Pat Slattery,**
  International Mentor, Author and Speaker

'Most people now listen to respond, not receive. They hover over words being said, picking up bits and pieces along the way, half-listening, sometimes thinking of other things until they resonate with an opportunity to add their bit, their opinions, advice, solutions, and thoughts. The loudness of that anticipated response can often silence what a person cannot convey in words...Allow the person to BE in that silence they may feel open to honest expression. Extend the silence and you can hear. Will you?'

- **Donna Kennedy,**
  7 times Bestselling Author, Speaker, Mentor and Psychologist

'In the healing of the broken child and the birthing of my true self I had the privilege of being a guest on the Fire in my Belly podcast.

During this very in depth and personal conversation I was giving the space to enter a place where I discovered my true purpose. I know that Pete Lonton helped unravel in me what my true calling was and it was a moment that I sat in true grace.'

- **Mary Keogh,**
  Founder Mary Keogh Life Mastery Academy

'I consider myself extremely lucky to have been given the opportunity to reflect on my life after a particularly challenging period. I also consider myself extremely lucky to have had the good fortune to meet the outstanding Pete Lonton and to be a guest on his Fire in the Belly podcast series in 2020. It genuinely was an amazing experience.'

- **Paul Coghlan,**
  Motivational Speaker and founder What I learned from Facing Cancer

'I suggest we understand our own voice first, before we listen to another's. Communication is essential, however the most important part of being heard is to first listen to yourself.'

- **Cliodhna Fullen,**
  Motivational Life Skills Mentor, is a well-known TV presenter / Director and Blogger

'It was, for me, one of those conversations of a lifetime. And yet it wasn't a conversation but Pete had gently, and with the great awareness that only a world-class mentor can bring, guided me through a conversation with myself.

In that conversation and through asking the next most obvious question I found clarity and through speaking my truth – confidence.'

- **Heather Shields,**
  Writer, Editor & Publisher

'I have been infamously private my entire life, sharing only what I've deemed necessary and closing down any further probing. To say my interview with Pete turned that on its head would be an understatement... My interview on Pete's podcast revealed more to me about myself than I had ever truly acknowledged; it allowed me to really dig deep on what had been holding me back becoming the best version of myself.'

- **Danielle Bell,**
  Hungry Mummy, Property Investor, Founder of Property Sourcing Made Simple

'Being on the Fire In The Belly podcast I definitely know I was being heard when Pete asked questions in relation to what I was saying that really made me think on a different level. It was like a breath of fresh air. Pete has a unique skill in the way he communicates with you and I have to say he is amazing.

I am quite a shy and reserved person who doesn't enjoy talking in public and certainly not about myself and my successes. He put me at ease right from the start and I was able to speak more openly and honestly than I think I ever have and felt safe in the process forgetting (thankfully) that there would be so many people being able to listen to my story.'

- **Lisa Stevenson,**
  Author of My Happy Minds Activity Journal and Founder Think Calm Be Calm

'You will never be heard if you don't know the lessons your inner genius wants to teach, and you will never know what your inner genius knows without Self-Reflection.'

- **Liam O'Neill,**
  The Prove-It Guy

'Life is strange, it presents opportunities at random times, often when you least expect them and you have to be ready to go with it. Every experience, every encounter, every time you get to share your passion and your voice for whatever it is that you do is step nearer to succeeding.'

- **Louisa Burnett**
  Artist

'Truly hearing, seeing or feeling someone is very rare. I'm not talking about hearing their voice or seeing their body. I'm talking about hearing and seeing the whole person: both what I call the Inner Game and the Outer Game, the feminine and the masculine, the shadow and the light, what we want to see, hear and feel and what we don't want to see, hear and feel. This is rare, because in order to do this, we need to see, hear and feel the entirety of ourselves. And yet, this is Mighty Pete's intention with Fire in the Belly.

- **Alexander Inchbald,**
  Extreme Artist, founder of Create Your Masterpiece,
  founder Masterpiece Movement, bestselling Author,
  Coach and founder WorldClass Academy.

'I have reflected a lot on being heard and sharing my story on Mighty Pete Lonton's Fire in the Belly podcast. I have shared my story on many forums but this was different.

If I was to give you words to describe it – profound, deep and interesting. I went to places in my mind I had avoided or at the very least not been vocal about. It was a therapeutic for me. I got a weight off my chest and in a positive, safe, constructive, non-judgmental environment. It truly was a great experience for me.'

- **Gary Doherty,**
  Founder Think Network and TEDxDerryLondonderry

'Being a guest on the Fire in the Belly show has been transformational for me. And not for the reasons you might think…this reflection began a journey of self-discovery that has changed so much in my life in a few short months.

I've gone and set new audacious life goals that I never would otherwise have considered. I have developed stronger relationships with my kids. I have attracted new clients to my business. My interview had the unintended consequence of forcing me to open my mind to new possibilities.'

- **Camilla Long,**
  Co-founder Bespoke Communications

'The Fire in the Belly Podcast and Pete Lonton are so different in the podcast world. Pete does an amazing job of truly listening, asking questions and truly holding space to hear the stories behind the answer and **Does. Not. Rush.**

Even after multiple grad degrees, certifications, and coaching and counseling others... Pete still tenderly touched my heart....because he actually listened. That's right! I got choked up on Fire in the Belly!'

- **Anne M Henderson,**
  Life Coach Annie, The Happy Mama Village Podcast,
  Coming Out Loved and Supported Podcast

'I believe I walked away from the interview with Pete, a different person. Someone with new awareness and gratitude that was released from within and if possible I felt a little lighter too! Pete has an incredible intuitive interview technique which captures authenticity, character and purpose in its purest form, from all his guests.'

- **Linda Carmichael,**
  CEO Make Me Mold Me

Book your Fire In The Belly Life Story Talk at

MightyPete.com

BE HEARD TO BE RICH

Recommended Books

There are many books that have influenced Be Heard To Be Rich and I have listed a number of them here. In my mid-30's it would be fair to say that I was not a reader but over the last few years, starting with Think and Grow Rich by Napoleon Hill, reading has become an essential part of my day.

Starting at 5.30am weekdays with my reading group we will read together for half an hour followed by a half hour discussion of the book. It has transformed how I read and experience books. I continue to learn with each read or re-read. The books listed here are amongst some of our favourites in the reading group.

The 'Happy Morning' reading group started at the beginning of a global lockdown in April 2020. We have a number of reading groups that meet during the day - and it is always 5.30am in some part of the world!

52 Recommended Books: One for Every Week of the Year

1. The Power Of Now - Eckhart Tolle
2. Ask!: The Bridge From Your Dreams To Your Destiny - Mark Victor Hansen and Crystal Dwyer Hansen
3. Psycho-Cybernetics - Maxwell Maltz, MD, FICS
4. Think and Grow Rich - Napoleon Hill
5. Limitless - Jim Kwik

6. The Complete 'Conversations With God' Series – Neale Donald Walsch
7. The Power of Imagination - Neville Goddard
8. Acres of Diamonds - Russell H. Conwell
9. Three Feet from Gold – Sharon Lechter and Greg Reid
10. The Confidence to Succeed - Donna Kennedy

11. BeLIFE or BeLIEf - Donna Kennedy, Pat Slattery, Heather Shields, Pete Lonton and Co-Authors
12. The Code of The Extraordinary Mind - Vishen Lakhiani
13. Ask and It is Given - Esther Hicks and Gerry Hicks
14. Unleash the Power Within - Tony Robbins
15. Stealing Fire - Jamie Wheal and Steven Kotler

16. The Values Factor - Dr John Demartini
17. The Secret - Rhonda Byrne
18. Who Moved My Cheese - Dr Spencer Johnson
19. Start With Why - Simon Sinek
20. Breaking the Habit of Being Yourself - Dr Joe Dispenza

21. The Science of Getting Rich - Wallace D. Wattles

22. Outwitting The Devil - Napoleon Hill and Sharon Lechter

23. Limitation is a Mirage - Liam O'Neill and Ian Rowland

24. Essentialism - Greg McKeown

25. The Success Principles - Jack Canfield

26. The Original Chicken Soup for the Soul - Jack Canfield, Mark Victor Hansen and Amy Newmark

27. Grit - Angela Duckworth

28. 12 Rules for Life - Jordan B. Peterson

29. The Magic of Thinking Big - David Schwartz PhD.

30. Rebel Ideas - Mathew Syed

31. The Compound Effect - Darren Hardy

32. Eat That Frog - Brian Tracy

33. Wishes Fulfilled – Dr Wayne Dyer

34. Scattered Minds – Gabor Maté MD.

35. Inspire Heal Empower – Jacqui Taaffe

36. The 7 Habits of Highly Effective People - Stephen Covey

37. The Warren Buffett Way – Robert G. Hagstrom

38. The Four Agreements – Don Miguel Ruiz

39. The Chimp Paradox – Prof Steve Peters

40. The 10X Rule – Grant Cardone

41. The 5 Second Rule – Mel Robbins

42. Life Leverage – Rob Moore

43. Rich Dad, Poor Dad – Robert T. Kiyosaki

44. The Alchemist – Paulo Coelho

45. Atomic Habits – James Clear

46. The Ultimate Jim Rohn Library – Jim Rohn
47. The Power of Your Subconscious Mind – Joseph Murphy
48. Be Water, My Friend – Shannon Lee
49. A New Earth – Eckhart Tolle
50. The Richest Man In Babylon – George S. Clason

51. Think and Sell Big – Christy Doherty
52. You Were Born Rich – Bob Proctor

Mighty Pete's Bucket List

The time is now – my 50 things to be, do and have over the
next 5-10 years.

1.	Teach my kids to drive	2.	Travel the world with my wife
3.	Dinner in The Treetop Restaurant	4.	Dive the Great Barrier Reef
5.	Run an Ultra Marathon	6.	Walk the length of Ireland
7.	Interview Oprah	8.	Set up my own TV and Audio Recording Studio
9.	Author / Co Author 100 books	10.	Interview Bob Proctor
11.	Set up Fire In The Belly Academy to help and inspire others	12.	Set up Fire In The Belly foundation for those in need
13.	Interview Will Smith	14.	Spend one year on a cruise ship travelling the world writing
15.	Hot Air Balloon ride	16.	Speak on stage in front of 1,000+ people
17.	Earn and Make $1,000,000 in 1 day	18.	Host an ongoing radio show
19.	Own one thousand investment properties	20.	Complete an Iron Man
21.	Row the Atlantic	22.	Walk the Great Wall of China
23.	Get a Tattoo	24.	Own a large villa in Spain with business conference facilities

25.	Walk the Camino De Santiago	26.	Build my own home
27.	Build a membership platform with 1,000,000 members	28.	Be awarded a Doctorate
29.	Build a healthy asset bank with passive income of $10,000,000 per annum	30.	Run the New York Marathon
31.	Bungee Jump	32.	Go white water rafting
33.	One year Spiritual Retreat	34.	Have my own personal chef and PA
35.	Stay in all of the accommodations in the Blue Book in Ireland	36.	Crew on a yacht race for 1 month+
37.	Give blood as often as possible	38.	Learn a new language
39.	Go on a Buddhist retreat	40.	Husky sledding adventure
41.	Stay in the Ice Hotel	42.	Sky Dive
43.	Have a large party and celebration for my 50th	44.	Go to the Straw Man festival
45.	Shoot an AK47	46.	Take part on a charity adventure
47.	Go on a Vietnam cycle challenge	48.	Rent a chalet and ski for 3 months

49. Visit the 7 Wonders of the World	50. Talk with my parents

Bucket List – My 50 things to be, do and have!

Mighty Pete's F*%k It List

What I do NOT want to be, do and have? 50 things I've let go…

1.	Not taking action I am in awe of.	2.	Rip the plaster off. If it feels wrong, looks wrong or smells wrong then it most likely is. Make a decision and pull the trigger!
3.	Common failure traits of deciding slowly and changing your mind quickly. Doing the opposite!	4.	The actions of others. Choose to stand out.
5.	It doesn't matter who's watching because you will always know, do it for you and have a clear conscious.	6.	Regrets!
7.	Worrying when good things don't happen – sometimes it's so that great things will.	8.	Not minding my F*%king language. If you say you are then you are.
9.	Not minding my thoughts! If you think you are then you are. Master your mindset.	10.	Thinking ifes a dress rehearsal. Waste it if you wish but the show will go on regardless!
11.	In the words of Pat Slattery, 'Other people's opinions are none of your business.'	12.	Carrying baggage it gets exponentially heavier the longer you carry it.

13.	Everyone farts! Get over it.	14.	People are not watching you 1/10 as much as you think they are. They're too busy watching themselves.
15.	The past is history. It's a mix of facts, beliefs and chosen memories.	16.	What if's.
17.	Likes on social media. 'You can't take likes to the bank.' — Alan Wallace	18.	Wondering about my life's purpose. The point is to find it.
19.	Losing my power. Reclaim your power! You have a bad habit and that is okay. You may have done some things wrong and that's okay — all that matters is what you do today.	20.	My ego - as much as I can, sometimes we need to get a big stepladder and get over ourselves.
21.	Not taking counsel from those with experience	22.	People's opinions — opinions are like bums, we all have one but it doesn't mean that we should show it.
23.	Bad diets!	24.	Not allowing my feelings and emotions.

25.	Sh1t that happens!	26.	Staying the same! Choosing your habits and ethics are the foundation blocks to creating lasting change.
27.	Not recognising my thoughts as thoughts that can be changed.	28.	Getting caught up in my emotions. We decide how we feel.
29.	Judgement – we are all good and bad. Some days more than others. Decide your intention.	30.	Need for acceptance – when you apply these rules you will likely outgrow those around you.
31.	Trying to change anyone – not your job.	32.	Thinking there's a right or a wrong.
33.	Judging others differently to myself.	34.	Not saying what I mean.
35.	Thinking life is happening to me. It's happening for me!	36.	Looking for a saviour. No one is coming to save us. Others can help but they can't do it for us. It's your job to help yourself. Put your big pants on and grow up.
37.	Thinking everyone has good intentions.	38.	Worry. It's a pointless reaction and doesn't solve anything.

39.	Waiting for an apology. Be the first to say sorry to others and never go to sleep on an argument.	40.	Coriander!
41.	'Never mind what anyone else thinks, just focus on what you think!' – David Lonton	42.	Not all that glistens is gold. Beware of false prophets.
43.	Thinking everyone has good intentions.	44.	Worry. It's a pointless reaction and doesn't solve anything.
45.	An inherited win will never be as sweet as an earned win.	46.	'Listening to the naysayers, it will dampen all of your dreams.' – Heather Shields
47.	Failure – it only becomes failure when you stop trying!	48.	Guilt - Use the ho'oponopono prayer for self-forgiveness; 'I'm sorry, please forgive me, thank you, I love you.'
49.	Saying the word sorry about myself! Start saying thank you – Change 'I can't' to 'I will' and 'I haven't' to 'I haven't yet!'	50.	Talking too much! 'Less said, soonest mended.' – Barney Hughes

51. Going too fast! Life is a journey not a destination. Slow doen and smell the roses. You are a walking miracle.	52. 'Yesterday's the past, tomorrow's the future, but today is a gift. That's why it's called the present.' – Bill Keane

F*%k It List - 50 things I don't need to experience! Ever (or ever again)

Letter to Your Future Self

A useful tool in hearing – and reaching – our riches is to write a letter to our future self. This is an opportunity to write from your wishes fulfilled.

Please use the template below and take time to write a letter to your future self a year from now!

Personal promise and commandment to future self;

I _____, on this date _____ [X   years from now] am so happy and grateful for my burning desire, passion, energy and focus.

I   have   now   achieved   _____

_____

_____with ease flow and   by _____
[goal completion date]

On the day, _____[insert todays date] I committed to focusing on this clear goal and followed it with unrelenting dedication and purpose.

Now   that   this   goal   has   been   achieved,   I   feel   _____

_____and   will

continue to grow and fulfil my vision mission and purpose.

I choose to be consistent and persistent in becoming the mightiest version of myself every single day.

I am so proud of me for listening to my inner genius, living with a Fire In The Belly and being true.

With love and joy

_____

[Sign] PS You're Awesome!!!

Epilogue

Is Your Inner Genius Being Heard?

Find Your Fire

Narrative TEDx Talk by Mighty Pete Lonton

TEDxDerryLondonderry February 2021

Have you ever found yourself at 2 am, sitting on the side of your bed, rocking backwards and forwards in the dark, not knowing what to do and what has happened? Well, that's where I found myself, and that I can tell you is a very dark place. I bring you back to today and where I am, and I have been through this amazing experience in this journey since that time. Inside that point of great overwhelm, has allowed me to do a lot more in my life.

I'm going to ask you a few questions.

First of all I'd like to ask;

What does fire in the belly mean to you?

Now, I'm not talking indigestion. I'm talking about that passion, that burning desire.

What does it really mean for you?

Do you just think we're all born with it?

Do you think all of us have it? And probably most importantly, what is your fire in the belly?

Having that opportunity to sit down with people is really something special. My name is Mighty Pete, also known as Pete Lonton. For me, I had the opportunity to go from being an engineer to where I am today. I'm lucky enough to be a podcaster, a mentor, a host, but most of all, being the host of the Fire In the Belly show.

Now you might ask what is the Fire In the Belly show. Well, it's something that has come about, really in a relatively short period of time, and has been extremely successful. It is all about sitting down in an interview style with guests. But what we're doing is providing a safe, pre-recorded space for people to come and share their lessons, their journey, their insights. Because believe it or not, we all have that passion and burning desire inside of us.

Now, to be successful means different things for different people.

And to be a guest on the show quite often we ask for that.

But success could be anything right?

It could be the fact of financial wealth. It could be goals achieved or could even be simply the fact that you're alive today. It is different for everyone. And that's okay, because being unique, is an amazing experience. The world would be a pretty weird place if we were all the same. *Why it really works?* Giving people the chance to sit down and talk about themselves, is something quite special. To be non-judgmental, to give that space and that opportunity to talk, and just be there.

In the show I like to actually sit down and ask lots of questions, but also we like to just give people the time. Then time after time we hear people saying, I haven't actually thought about that before, or that's something I'm not sharing publicly. Not that we necessarily want to try and divulge personal secrets. It's just that, despite this being in a world where we're more and more connected and all the social media, yet, the noise and everything going on around us means we don't actually hear ourselves! We don't care our own genius; we don't hear what's going on.

The opportunity to sit down with somebody, and actually walk a mile in their shoes can be something incredibly enlightening. Because you suddenly have a newfound respect for what they do and where they are, and when they talk about their passion, whatever it may be, they exude an energy that is absolutely embracing and enticing for all.

I want to take you back to that night, sitting on that bed at 2am, rocking backwards and forwards. Well, that, quite simply, was tooth ache. Now tooth ache is something a lot of us have had, and it's nothing that unusual. But as you know when it's bad enough that tooth ache is something that feels absolutely connected to every bone in your body. The nerves and what it set off overwhelmed me, not knowing what to do feeling for me it was really just something I couldn't take anymore. Thankfully, the following morning I was able to secure an emergency appointment with my dentist. Right enough they turned around and confirmed that yes, there was a problem with my tooth. Unfortunately at that time, it was two days before Christmas, and further treatment was not possible for another two weeks. Well when you've got to that stage in your life, when actually enough is enough, then you realise something has to change. That point of great overwhelm has to bring a point of great change. So I decided that one of two things was going to happen, either the dentist was going to remove my tooth, or I was.

Now after a little bit of nervous laughter, the dentist realised I was deadly serious. I'm happy to confirm that after 15 minutes, against advice and with the waiver signed, my tooth was indeed removed. To have that tooth in my hand, and to have it away, was actually one of the most enlightening experiences. Now of course the tooth was also a metaphor for what was going on. Getting that out of my mouth, getting it away from me, it actually signified what was really going on. That ability to just have that change, when enough was enough and things have to change to go forward.

Sometimes, really in life, you have to take time out! For me at that time, I was 37 and a half years of age. So, statistically, I suppose I was at the midpoint in my life - call it a midlife crisis if you wish, I don't mind. *But I had to ask myself, if I was to replay the second half of my life, the same way I'd travelled the first half of my life, then would I be happy with this?*

Well, in some ways, yes, and I'm extremely grateful for everything that I've had in my life. But I had this little scratch and voice in my mind, saying, *Am I capable of more? Do you have more potential? I would ask you all, are you capable of more. Do you have more potential?*

Well the answer that came back from the little voice in my head, said yes you are.

So slowly but surely I decided to start asking the question, *What if? What if I tried a little bit more? What if I asked a different question? What if I spoke to somebody who had been successful or achieved something that I haven't? What if, what if I took 1% of my day, only 14.4 minutes a day, to do something new or different?*

Well, I can now happily report, amazing things do happen!

From that point of starting to ask what if?, I came to the decision that it would be really nice to sit down and talk to people about their changes and their life stories.

So I started to ask myself, *What is this fire in the belly? What makes somebody passionate? What makes somebody jump out of bed and want to take over the world, when the next person wants to jump out of bed and turn on the TV?* We're all born naked and screaming. We're all similar flesh and blood, but yet people achieve different things.

So I wanted to know the formula, because my formula was wrong.

So, taking time to sit down with people. One of the first conversations I had was with my brother-in-law. We sat down and I asked him what 'fire in the belly' meant to him. Some two and a half hours later, we were deep in conversation, and had to pull ourselves away to go and collect kids from school. But what that proved to me, almost instantly, is that actually we all have a passion, and we might hear it if we take the time to sit down and listen.

Now why does the Fire In The Belly show and listening process work? Well, the listening process is something that really has evolved with me. I believe we all have a story. I personally believe we all have a 'fire in the belly'. As long as you have a beat in your heart, and air in your lungs, I believe you have a passion and you have a potential. By sitting down, allowing people to just talk, talk without judgement, without fear, just allowing them to be themselves in a safe space, but in a positive cathartic way, it has a certain magic and it is amazing when you talk to guests, you would be surprised by how many people say they have rarely, if ever, had the chance to actually do that. In this world where we're so digitally connected, it's also strange when people say they're not being heard.

Fast forward to today, we've been lucky enough to have nearly 400 guests come on to the show and go through the Life Story Talk interview.

And that is something that has taught me a huge amount. That ability to sit down with people and talk about their passions, because when someone talks about their passions it's absolutely magnetic. Suddenly you find your passion in similar things. I found myself getting passionate about certain things that I know nothing about, simply because the guest has actually exuded that energy.

By sitting down and learning, that really has taught me so much. That ability to learn and have passion. So far we've been lucky enough to have everything from auditors to people who are going through and learning about anthropology. We've had change makers to cake makers. We have people who are shark whisperers to sex educationalists and coaches. This is such a variety of people and it's amazing, their uniqueness. When you get to sit down with guests and learn about their passion, their Fire In The Belly, it truly is something quite special.

Two of the questions I like to ask on the show, and I would ask you now are; *Do you like yourself? And do you love yourself?*

Now, quite often people will very quickly see the egotistical side and say well 'I don't love myself'. But it's actually a very serious question when you sit down and think about it. What I have found on the show is that approximately 30% of the interviews will never be aired. Partly because we do provide a pre-recorded space so that people can listen back first and have the story that they want in the public. But I have found that the people who generally cannot answer the question whether they like themselves and love themselves, quite often they're the interviews that are not broadcast to air. Sometimes it is because it becomes too emotional, or there are certain things in their past they don't want to share, or sometimes that little voice in their head, their little genius realises that certain things aren't resolved for them. So it's really quite amazing when you actually take the time to listen.

So whilst some 30% of interviews aren't actually broadcast, they serve a purpose in allowing people to move forward. And that's something I love to do, to sit down with people and help them to find their passion, find their Fire In The Belly and really move forward.

I would ask you now, *What are you doing to find your passion? Do you live in your spirit of what you are? Have you found the flame inside you? Have you taken the time to listen?* Whether it is 60 minutes, two hours or three hours make sure you listen, listen with a blank canvas. Listen with only a question or the ability to not judge. Just to be able to hear what each other, wants to say.

We're all perfectly imperfect, and that's okay. I'm incredibly fortunate to be able to sit with people and my guilty pleasure is to hear other people's stories because indeed that reflection allows us to see more in ourselves.

So I'd really encourage everyone to take time for you, take time to Know yourself. Find your passion and be the best version, the mightiest version of yourself. I am Mighty Pete and I thank you very much.

BE HEARD TO BE RICH

12 Commandments of Listening

1. Learning is done by listening and the more you learn the more you earn. So why not listen more to earn more?

2. You can't shake a hand whilst waving a fist. You also cannot hear properly if you're too busy talking. Two ears versus one mouth is a convenient ratio to apply.

3. There is power in the pauses. Silence is the space where words are held. Embrace the space and the silence as fertile ground for the seeds of thoughts.

4. Words are perfectly imperfect, and that's okay. Sometimes they're the best thing we have to describe the indescribable. Being speechless and words failing are expressions that we often hear when people are at the point of overwhelm.

5. Listening is connecting. It can be an expression of love.

6. Words cannot be unsaid. It is when we consider why they were said that we can perhaps begin to truly hear the meaning. If we accept that things happen for a reason then the power and purpose of words can be realised.

BE HEARD TO BE RICH

12 Commandments of Listening

7. Know that you don't know; listen to hear not reply.

8. The truth is a live ecosystem, and is often just something that hasn't been disproven yet.

9. Rest assured, your subconscious mind, which runs your body and mind, is smarter than the smartest conscious person in the world. When's the last time you told your heart to beat, cells to regrow or sense a threat?

10. Call a person a fool long enough and they surely will become one. 'Learned helplessness' is when we have been taught or trained not to help ourselves.

11. Mind your F*%king Language. Sticks and stone can hurt your bones, but words can scar you for life. There's as much power in negatives as positives but very different outcomes.

12. Your truth and opinion are just that, they are yours! Be mindful that You cannot walk a lifetime in another person's shoes.

About the Author

'I have a question for you - when was the last time someone gave you the opportunity to talk without judgement in a safe space and in a positive way?'

Mighty Pete Lonton

Mighty Pete Lonton is a Bestselling Author, Fire In The Belly Show Host, Podcaster, Entrepreneur, Mentor, TEDx Speaker, Property Investor, Husband and Father of three beautiful girls.

Pete's background is in project management and property, but his true passion is the 'Fire In The Belly' Show and project which he started in February 2020. In its first year, Pete has spent over 1,000 hours listening to some 400 people share their life stories on the show. His mission is to hear others with the intention to help them find their potential and become the mightiest version of themselves.

The 'Fire In The Belly' Project was born after the death of both his parents, suffering through periods of depression, a business downturn, career burn-out, and ultimately what he now considers his years spent not stoking his 'Fire In The Belly.' In 2017, at 37.5 years of age, Pete went through a huge change in his life, he found his Fire in the Belly and he is now on a journey of learning, growing, accepting, and inspiring others. Pete can connect with people and intuitively ask questions to reveal a person's passion and discover how they can live their mightiest life. The true power of 'Fire in The Belly' is the Q&A's – Questions and Actions!

Book your Fire In The Belly Life Story Talk at MightyPete.com

Fire In The Belly Show & Podcast

Available on YouTube, Omnify, Apple, Spotify

Join the Fire In The Belly Online Community

Facebook: Fire In The Belly

YouTube: Fire In The Belly

Instagram: @mightypetelonton

LinkedIn: Mighty Pete Lonton

Printed in Great Britain
by Amazon